T0274725

panam.captain

panam.captain

timothy mellon

Skyhorse Publishing

Skyhorse Publishing books may be purchased in bulk at special discounts for sales promotion, corporate gifts, fund-raising, or educational purposes. Special editions can also be created to specifications. For details, contact the Special Sales Department, Skyhorse Publishing, 307 West 36th Street, 11th Floor, New York, NY 10018 or info@skyhorsepublishing.com.

Visit our website at www.skyhorsepublishing.com.
Please follow our publisher Tony Lyons on Instagram @tonylyonsisuncertain.

10 9 8 7 6 5 4 3 2 1

Library of Congress Cataloging-in-Publication Data is available on file.

Print ISBN: 978-1-5107-8034-7
eBook ISBN: 978-1-5107-8035-4

Cover design by Brian Peterson

Printed in the United States of America

Contents

Table of Figures

Preface

I will tell you in a few words why I decided to write this book:

First, when you are having fun in life, you keep thinking, "Gee, if only I had time to sit down and record what has just happened! It would be fun to read about it later and to describe it to other people." Of course, one never has the time, nor can afford to make the time, to commit these thoughts to paper.

Second, one hopes that someone else can be convinced to make the effort. But then that person's point of view won't be quite the same, and chances are some critical points will either be omitted or described in a way that misses a basic point.

Third, none of us is getting any younger. *Tempus fugit*! And memories have a way of waning (which in some instances can actually be a good thing). The longer one waits to record a thought, the less likely will be the accuracy of the description.

Fourth, I never thought I would have the discipline or patience to actually organize and transcribe all the matters that I thought might be worth preserving. That is, until I just sat down and started. When I discovered how easy it was for me to write, I said to myself, "Well, better do it now, do it right, and get it done."

This book was not ghost-written: every single word is my own. I have enjoyed the process, and may now have enough confidence to go on to write about other things. We'll see.

—Tim Mellon

CHAPTER I

KID FROM PITTSBURGH

My name is Timothy Mellon. Please call me Tim. I was born in Pittsburgh, Pennsylvania on July 22, 1942. I remained in Pittsburgh for four days and was then whisked off to my family's new home in Virginia. And that was probably a good thing, as Pittsburgh's atmosphere was none too healthy in 1942.

My parents lived in a brand new Georgian-style house in Upperville, Virginia. It was (and still is) situated on a lovely farm of several thousand acres in "horse country." Rolling hills interspersed with clumps of woods and punctuated by several man-made ponds. Fox hunting was the social activity of highest importance, and both my mother and father enjoyed the chase.

My maternal grandparents from Kansas City would visit from time to time, the Conovers. Dr. Charles Conover was a descendant of the Dutch Van Kovenhoven family that emigrated to the New World in the 17th century. They landed on Long Island and, generation-by-generation, moved Westward with the opportunities. Charles Conover was always with his pipe, booming loud with his infectious sense of humor. Pearl, his wife, was a dour soul. She rarely spoke and often had an uncomfortable expression on her face.

My Granny Nora lived in Connecticut but visited less often. She was the daughter of the McMullen brewers from Hertfordshire, North of London, and charmed my grandfather Andrew into marriage, a tale best described by David Cannadine in his biography *Mellon*.[1] Andrew Mellon I never met, as he died long before I was born.

Figure 1: With the Conovers.

What I remember of the first few years of my life consists of unrelated snippets. I am told that my older sister Cathy did not speak to me for the first five years of my life; now I think I should be thankful. I remember evenings in the Jeffersonian-style garden with serpentine brick walls. I remember Frau Kruger, the governess, making me sit for what seemed like hours undoing the knot I had tied in the pull string of my pajamas. (When I grew older, I assumed that Frau Kruger was a German agent, planted by the Nazis to make our lives miserable.)

And I distinctly remember that day I was taking my nap after lunch. The radio was on. The newscaster announced that an atomic bomb had been dropped on Japan. I was just three years old, and obviously didn't understand the import of the news. But I remember it vividly.

Then I remember the day that Captain Vaughn, my father's friend from the Army (they both served together in the OSS in England)[2] took me in the Jeep to the depot in Rectortown. There awaited a steam locomotive heading a short freight train. I was invited aboard the cab to take a ride to Front Royal, courtesy of Harry deButts, at that time President

1 David Cannadine, *Mellon* (New York: Alfred A. Knopf, 2006).

2 James K. Vaughn later served with Kermit Roosevelt in Iran at the time of the overthrow of Mohammad Mosaddeq.

of the Southern Railway. Mr. deButts also lived in Upperville. What a thrill for a four-year-old! I burned my finger slightly from touching the firebox. What I didn't know at the time was that the excursion was a diversion. My mother had just died from a heart attack brought on by asthma, and it was deemed better that I miss the funeral.

After that, my father was often away. He enrolled in a classics course at St. John's College in Maryland, I think to take his mind off the sadness. He would occasionally travel to Switzerland, where I presume he met with Dr. Carl Jung. Dr. Jung helped my mother earlier in her quest to overcome her allergies, which she was convinced were based on psychological factors. What I remember is the strawberry jam in tubes (like toothpaste) that he would bring back from Switzerland.

Less than a year later, my father re-married. Bunny had recently divorced Stacy Lloyd. They had lived across the Blue Ridge Mountain in Millwood. Bunny had helped design the Jeffersonian garden for my mother. She brought her two children, Stacy and Eliza, to Upperville to live. All of a sudden I had a stepsister three months younger than myself, and my sister gained a stepbrother three months her senior. Eliza and I were called "The Little Ones". The Little Ones were six years younger than the Big Ones. The four children all got along well with one another.

Jimmy Vaughn had helped me set up my first Lionel train set on the living room floor of the Brick House. Later, when we moved into the original Oak Spring farmhouse, I was clever enough to set them up myself. I had also received a fancy Zenith clock radio, with alarm, for Christmas. In the back of the radio was a socket into which one could plug any 110-volt household device. I decided I would plug the transformer for my train set into the back of this radio. "You can't do that!" yelled my stepmother, "You'll burn down the house!" She was not convinced by my assurances that this was a safe procedure; she called Gene Caylor, the farm electrician, for expert advice. "Yes, Mrs. Mellon, it's

OK if Tim plugs the train set into the radio." Vindicated! I'm not sure our relationship was quite the same forever after. Lesson of Life: Don't back down from your firm beliefs.

While I'm on the subject of Oak Spring, I am reminded of the Cabbage, a porcelain artifact that graced our dining room table for decades (see Figure 2). When a sibling would ask for, say, the bread to be passed, another would start to pass it over the cabbage, which would elicit the automatic shriek of "Don't pass that over the cabbage, it's a priceless antique!" Of course, we learned to feint such an action just to be treated with the response! My stepmother, however, had the last word. Her only bequest to me after her death in 2014 at the age of 103 was the Cabbage. It now graces our sideboard.

Figure 2: The cabbage.

We were ruled by a series of governesses from various lands: Switzerland, Norway, and England. Occasionally, Ms. Charleston from the United States would relieve the regular governess for a vacation. Ms. Charleston was not as sweet as the others. Eliza and I would conspire to list nasty tricks which we could play on her, but of course neither of us ever had the nerve to launch one of them.

Childhood summers consisted of vast stretches of time spent at the swimming pool in Virginia. The Fourth of July was the occasion for a huge picnic by the pool. My forte was swimming underwater; my unbeaten (by siblings) record was four laps of the pool. My stepbrother Stacy (nicknamed Tuffy) was forever being reprimanded for doing cannonballs into the pool. He got into even hotter water when he threw a cherry bomb into the pool, causing severe damage to the underwater light.

Middle of July became the time to move on to the cooler climes of Cape Cod. I am convinced that Global Warming was actually born in Virginia: I can remember day-after-day of 100-plus degree temperatures in the early 1950s. Hot, humid, and miserable. In Cape Cod, we rented for several years before building a summer residence. The second year there we rented a house two doors down from the Oyster Harbors Club, a fancy golf venue. We took many of our dinners at the Club. One day my siblings decided to terrorize the household: they threw scads of comic books, nicely soaked in water, down the stairwell to the consternation of the grown-ups. But I was INNOCENT!

CHAPTER II

SCHOOL DAYS

In the fall of 1947, Eliza and I went off to kindergarten at Miss Collier's house in Middleburg. Bob Butler, the family chauffeur, drove us in one of those nice Plymouth station wagons with sides made of real wood. Miss Collier's kindergarten was on Route 50, just opposite the Dimos residence, on the way into town. Allegedly, ten or so of us learned to get along. As I recall, the entire class graduated and moved into the first grade at Hill School, a private primary school in the same town. Our good friends Helen Dimos, Stuart Saffer, Linda Nachman, and Patty Connors were all in the same class.

Global Cooling struck the same year. A blizzard enveloped Northern Virginia and the county roads were impassable for several days. Route 623 that bisected our farm was still a dirt road then, and even after it had been plowed, it became a treacherous muddy quagmire of sloppy red Virginia clay. But Bob Butler saw us through.

I spent grades one through four at Hill School and enjoyed it very much. Miss Anne Goughenhauer was our first grade teacher (all subjects, including spelling, arithmetic, French, and music). She was a *Grande Dame* and commanded total respect from her flock.

Then, in fourth grade, having made all these new friends at Hill, my parents decided that it would be a good idea if I went away to boarding school. My father took me to look at Eaglebrook in Western Massachusetts and the Fenn School in Concord, outside of Boston. He settled on Fenn. I suspect now that the reason was to provide himself cover so as to be able to visit Valerie Churchill when he came up from Virginia occasionally to take me out for the weekend. She had been a nurse in Scotland during the War, and cared for my father when he had been evacuated from France with a severe case of pneumonia. She moved to Boston after the War and lived in an apartment overlooking the Charles River Basin.

So in the Fall of 1952, I trundled up to Boston on the night train and found my new home in the Farm House, a dormitory of three floors mastered by David McLean. The first semester I roomed with Harry Lane, a nasty little boy from South Carolina. We got along grudgingly.

School went well, and I was able to develop my talents in making model airplanes. Initially, I built my own design of a high-wing Cessna-like single engine. It really was just a glider, 8-inch wingspan, with a die in the nose to simulate the weight of an engine. When complete, I took it up to the third-floor bathroom in the Farm House and launched it on its maiden flight out over the main football field. It glided perfectly in large circles down to a safe landing. I was elated!

Some days later, I had stored this model airplane in my sports locker during football practice. When I returned from the field, I discovered that my model had been smashed inside the locker. I was devastated. I have always suspected that mean Harry Lane. He left Fenn at the end of that semester. Lessons of life: don't leave your valuables unsecured.

Fenn School was a mile from the center of Concord, the town made famous by the ride of Paul Revere. We walked to town every Saturday to buy candy at the Country Store. I loved those mouth-searing round Red Hot Hot Balls. Eventually I saved enough allowance to purchase a beautiful Raleigh bicycle. I remember it costing $96. I turned the handlebars upside down to make it look like one of those cool racing bikes.

We were allowed complete freedom to ride our bicycles around the countryside, alone, as there was no fear in the early 1950s of kidnappers or molesters. I remember riding all the way to Carlyle, and to Hanscom Air Force Base in Bedford. Fenn School taught responsibility by trusting their wards to act in a responsible manner.

One Sunday evening in the Fall of 1952 some of us were tossing a football around in the grassy area between the buildings. The monotonous drone of airplanes captured our attention. Looking up, we saw a flight of dozens and dozens of fighter planes approaching, all in formation, heading West. They seemed to be at about 4,000 feet. I am sure they were heading off to the Korean War. I have never since seen such a stirring sight.

Fenn was situated only a mile from the departure end of Runway 29 at Hanscom. Classes would frequently be interrupted by the deafening sound of a departing F-89 Scorpion. We were all ecstatic because class would have to come to a grinding halt for several minutes until the roar subsided. One day a new B-47 Strategic Bomber took off along the same flight path. Also a staggering sight.

Sua Sponte was Fenn's motto: On Your Own Initiative, roughly translated. I learned what this meant after an 18-inch snowfall in the Winter of 1954. I awoke early, excited to see such an even blanket covering the grounds. I rushed to get dressed, way before breakfast. Finding a shovel, I started to clear the main paths between the school buildings. The task was daunting, but the wooden walkways put down each Fall by Eddy Cullinane, the school janitor, made the pathways very easy to find. Kudos rained down. I felt very proud for having made the effort, on my own and without anyone's prodding.

Fenn was organized on the trimester system, so that exams were out of the way at the beginning of the main vacations (Christmas, Easter, and Summer). Thanksgiving was a special case. My stepbrother Stacy, who attended Middlesex School close by, would travel back to Virginia on the same train. One year we could not find seats on the entire train until we reached Baltimore. I learned that a train ticket did not entitle you to a seat, but only to the transportation itself.

Roger Fenn was the Founder and Headmaster of the Fenn School. He lived in a large white house up on a hillock opposite the Farm House. He taught some of us about banding birds and appreciating wildlife. His wife Eleanor taught French, and I suffered under her tutelage in the seventh grade. She was short, squat, and frankly somewhat difficult to appreciate. Our class was held in a half-basement room, by which I mean that outside ground level was about four feet above the classroom floor. One spring day, with all the windows open, a cat appeared on one of the window sills. Startled, Mrs. Fenn began ranting, "*Allez chat, allez!*" We sat in stunned silence for several minutes.

Every Fenn student was required to take a course in carpentry. The shop was run by Charles Ward, a crusty old New Englander. As we approached our Senior year, we began to notice that Mr. Ward was in the habit of refolding his luncheon paper napkin, once in half and then again, before inserting it into his jacket pocket. What frugality! The students began to refer to him surreptitiously as "Cheap Charlie". We resolved to bring this foible to the World's attention. In Cheap Charlie's own shop, several students set about building a cubic box out of plywood, three feet in each dimension. The hinged top had a cut-out with a piece of mesh to prevent escape of the contents. Meanwhile, the entire Senior class began saving their napkins, folding them in the time-honored fashion, and dropping them eventually into the finished plywood container. At Commencement, we presented the box to Cheap Charlie Ward, chock-a-block full of napkins, as a going-away gift from the Class of 1956.

My education at Fenn was interrupted twice by visits to the Massachusetts Eye and Ear Infirmary in Boston. First visit was for the purpose of draining an infected ear; second time was to have my tonsils removed. I took an instant loathing to the stench of the ether used as the anesthetic. Long gone now is the array of flashing neon advertising signs across the Charles River in Cambridge. They were my entertainment after lights-out. My father would visit me, of course.

Some summers during grade school I had the opportunity to work on the family farm. After preparing my own breakfast and lunch box, I would bicycle about a mile to the Rokeby side of the farm. First year my job was to fill the watering troughs for the horses and cattle. Walk and wait, walk and wait. . . . I learned something about patience, as each trough took about fifteen minutes to fill.

In subsequent years I graduated to driving a tractor, mowing the pastures with a Massey-Ferguson and sickle-bar mower. The first time I mowed the 40-acre field, it took me three days. Later I would rake the windrows of alfalfa for baling. Then stack the bales on the trailer to be transported to the barn. These periods of work would usually come to an abrupt halt when poison ivy or poison oak broke out all over my arms.[1]

I graduated from Fenn in 1956 and moved across town to Milton Academy for the four year High School stint. Some other Fenn students came along to Milton, but none have remained as close as my original Hill School buddies. Milton had more rules and favored their students with less trust. This led to students testing those rules and often being

1 Many years later, having become convinced of the efficacy of the use of Vitamin C to mitigate the effects of the common cold, as propounded by Dr. Linus Pauling, I attempted the same regimen with respect to poison ivy: 1000 milligrams of Vitamin C per hour had the effect of drying up the rash quite rapidly (half the normal time) and considerably reducing the itching. Tecnu is also an effective product, if applied immediately after exposure.

subject to the inevitable discipline for infractions. Smoking was prohibited. So we found hideouts in which to smoke. TVs were not allowed. So senior year I built a chest out of plywood to hide a TV in my closet. It even had two holes through which the telescoping rabbit ear antennae could be raised. I assume that the only reason we weren't "caught" in senior year was the coincidental Fund Raising Campaign that was designed to appeal to the parents.

Freshmen were relegated to cubicles on the top floor of the dormitory, in our case Wolcott House. As serfs, we were assigned duties by the Housemaster such as yelling the wake-up call and waiting on tables. I had the distinct honor of occupying the same cubicle on the wall of which T. S. Eliot had carved his name. Sunday evenings, we freshmen would gather in the floor-master's living room to be read a story. I remember most C. S. Forester's *The Gun*.

In the Autumn of my sophomore year, I contracted the Asian flu, just in time to miss a trip home to Virginia coinciding with the visit of Queen Elizabeth to my family's farm. They had race horses in common. Bummer. The following spring, however, I was invited to the Bahamas for Spring Vacation by my friend Chas Freeman. His father ran the Royal Victoria Hotel, which had undergone labor difficulties of an existential magnitude. Years later I would appreciate his predicament. Nonetheless, I was able to embarrass myself beyond my greatest expectations by falling through, and ruining, the Plexiglas windshield of his zippy speedboat. He was most gracious about the incident.

I was also invited to go on a tour of Europe the following summer (1958) with Chas and four students from another prep school, led by their teacher Art Claridge. My father subsidized Chas's trip, I suppose as a way to make up for the broken windshield. England, Belgium, Netherlands, Germany, Switzerland, Austria, Italy, and France, all in a minibus. We were more interested in the girls we had met on the *Queen Elizabeth* on the voyage over, than in the museums and cathedrals presented to us. I was not amused when one of the group, in Venice, left a dead fish in my suitcase. We spent much of the time in Paris playing the pinball machines at the Whoopy Club. Chas claimed to have scored with the barmaid, but I later learned to discount much of his bravado. I befriended a girl from Durham, North Carolina, Sally Hobbs. She was travelling with her family through France, where her father had fought in WWII. Marcus Hobbs was a Professor of Chemistry and Provost at Duke University. I learned later that he had been involved in developing methods for tracking gunfire hits by pilots firing at towed targets. He was also instrumental in developing the Research Triangle in North Carolina.

Looking back on my high school years, I believe that travel became perhaps the most important component of my education. Milton Academy had a rigorous curriculum, but the courses offered seemed to be drab and unexciting. I did enjoy the extracurricular courses I was able to take, such as Mechanical Drawing from Mr. Williams, the shop teacher, advanced calculus from Mr. Herzog, and especially the beginning Italian course put on by Mr. Pocock and Mr. Daley. "*Buon giorno!*" "*Buon giorno!*" "*Como sta Lei?*" "*Molto bene, molto bene, grazie!*"

The following summer (1959) I travelled again, this time to Munich to live with a German family with the goal of learning how to speak German. Dr. August Reis (a friend of my family's doctor in New York, André Kling) had me as a guest in his house for six weeks. Dr. Reis was a research doctor, convinced that any illness could be detected and identified simply by using external non-invasive measurements. He and his wife Mary enjoyed food, and it showed. I did learn some German, mostly from a tutor they had arranged, but I learned much about the culture too. Every weekend he would whisk us off to some fascinating destination: Augsburg and the Black Forest, an Austrian castle, the city of Salzburg, Nürnberg or the blood sausage restaurant associated with the brewery in Aying (North of Munich). Once on the Autobahn at the gentle speed of 145 clicks, his Mercedes had a rear tire blowout. Luckily there was very little traffic in those days.[2]

I returned directly to Virginia, where I purchased my first car from Deering Chevrolet: a beautiful blue 1960 Chevrolet BelAir four door sedan. I attended a community dance shortly afterwards at Buchanan Hall in Upperville. Music by Chauncey Brown. I met Susan Tracy that evening: she was a friend of Wendy Whitney, a Hill School friend two years my senior, and was staying at Wendy's house on Route 50. They had both attended Madeira School together. Being as how I was quite attracted to Ms. Tracy, I asked her on a movie date in my brand new Chevy. She accepted, and the following evening we drove across the mountain to the Winchester drive-in. I don't honestly remember the movie except that Joan Crawford may have been starring in it. What I do remember is that Sue smoked Pall Mall cigarettes. The Chevy had a pull-down ashtray, with the ash receptacle on the left side and a lighter on the right side. To my utter horror, my date was flicking ashes into, then extinguishing her cigarette in the cup-shaped bowl beneath the lighter, instead of into the ash receptacle. My brand new car, despoiled! Lesson of Life: Bite your tongue, especially when it really doesn't matter that much. . . .

Sue and I quickly became good friends. By Thanksgiving, I had flown down to Newark to meet her family in Morristown. Her father, Osgood Tracy,[3] was at that time president of Esso. He was able to enjoy

2 Some years later, my wife Sue (see below) and I visited the Reis family at their new home outside of Munich. One evening, they entertained a few additional guests, including one Ernst "Putzi" Hanfstaengl. Putzi had been a confidant to Hitler, played the piano for him on occasion, and hid Hitler in his house after the Beer Hall Putsch. "But I am American!" Putzi proclaimed, "My mother was a Sedgwick!" Sue piped up "Well, I'm a Sedgwick too." File this bit of trivia under "Small World".

3 "Otz" to his friends. Aptly described as "Seldom in error, never in doubt!"

The Tracys employed a wonderful housekeeper, Minnie Harris from Baton Rouge. Salt of the Earth. One day Sue was trying to wrest from her the recipe for some sweet rolls. "How much sugar do you use, Minnie?" **"Oh, 'bouta mouf-full."**

the irony of his youngest daughter dating a Gulf Oil type. I had to laugh one time when his chauffeur complained that his limousine failed due to water in the gasoline. Yes, Esso gasoline. It became a family joke. By the end of Christmas vacation Sue and I agreed to be engaged. My secondary education was coming to an end, and I was preparing for college. A tempestuous time, all in all.

Sue was enrolled at Bryn Mawr College, West of Philadelphia. I saw obvious advantages of trying to enroll at Haverford, several miles away. But my father, a keen Yalie, had different notions. He quite insisted that Yale would provide a far superior education and that I would avoid the provincial atmosphere offered by a college like Haverford. I demurred. After all, I had this neat Chevy that could make the trip from New Haven to Bryn Mawr in less than four hours. No big deal.

The more important tempest dealt with our engagement. I announced my intentions to my father whilst enroute to Kuwait on a junket that had been arranged by Gulf Oil and Kermit Roosevelt. They had rented a commercial BEA Viscount to tour the Mideast. I cornered my father in the forward cabin on one leg of the flight and explained my intentions to marry. Even though I was only a Yale freshman at the time, he seemed to have no particular objection, and expressed happiness that I had found someone special. But upon our return to the US, after he had talked with my stepmother, the (you-know-what) hit the fan. In no uncertain terms, I should not get married until having graduated from Yale. They invited the Tracys to dinner in New York and tried to convince them to kibosh the notion. I learned only after fifty years, from Sue's older sister Sally, that my stepmother went so far as to tell the Tracys "This girl simply will not do!" Otz Tracy was so enraged that he could not bear to relate this to either of us.

Much stress ensued (no pun intended). The Tracy parents were solidly on our side, and I felt immediately and completely accepted into the family. Next March, they took us to Antigua for spring vacation. We stayed at the Mill Reef Club, just a stone's throw away from the house that my parents had just finished building on the hill overlooking Half Moon Bay. We forged ahead to plan a wedding for June 1963, at the end of my junior year at Yale. My parents finally relented to the accelerated schedule, but only with extreme grudge.

CHAPTER III

YALE

In spite of the obvious distractions of a wonderful engagement, I plodded ahead into the Yale undergraduate curriculum. Advanced Placement tests allowed me to avoid all courses in English Literature, a complete fill of which I had experienced at Milton Academy. I thought first of languages, taking a course in German, then in summer school a course in Spanish. Not particularly satisfying, I concluded. I headed toward Political Science, and eventually majored in that "discipline". I enjoyed various odd-ball courses such as Science I (Geology the first semester of freshman year, taught by Rocky Flint [I swear, that was his name], then Meteorology the second semester) and Latin American History. I learned Bolivar's famous quip: "Introducing Democracy to the Americas is as useful as plowing the oceans." I was a B student, for the most part, but was totally humiliated to receive a D in the first semester of Psychology. At least this was better than my friend Dick Morcroft's 35 percent on his first Economics 101 test.

Weekends were spent commuting to Bryn Mawr, or escorting my *fiancée* around New Haven, enjoying events like football games and the Ray Charles concert in Woolsey Hall. My friend Chas had met a girl from Holyoke at a mixer, and they also became fast friends. One weekend, I was prevailed upon to go to Chas's aunt and uncle's house in New Canaan for dinner. I was the chauffeur in my still vinyl-scented 1960

Chevy BelAir. On the return trip I sensed some unusual commotion in the rear bench seat. I feared yet another despoliation of my beautiful chariot.

When applying to Yale, I had asked to be paired with a German-speaking student, so as to hopefully improve my language skills. Yale offered up Dieter. Dietrich Brand was from Braunschweig in Germany. His father ran a profitable felt manufacturing business. Dieter was made my roommate during the first semester, but his studies suffered immediately from the many distractions, and he asked to be allowed into a single room.

After freshman year, Dieter and I were placed in the same suite in Trumbull College, along with Chas Freeman and Dick Morcroft. Dieter became distracted again, and fell behind in his weekly essays in his Classical Civilization course. We set up an assembly line: Dieter offered the theme, Chas whipped out the language, and I typed the final drafts on my new IBM Selectric typewriter. I remember especially Dieter's theme entitled "A Friend in Need is a Friend Indeed".

Junior year allowed us to all move into single rooms. Chas had moved off campus, having married Pat Trenery, his mixer date. But along came the Cuban Missile Crisis, just as we were settling into serious uninterrupted study. Dieter's family business had a subsidiary in Toronto. Dieter became convinced that he could survive the certain rain of ballistic missiles headed towards the US by driving his Volkswagen bug from New Haven cross-country to a plot of land his family owned North of Toronto. His VW had a winch, to pull himself out should he become stuck in the mud on the way. Dieter packed gallon jars of salt, flour, and sugar to bury on the land in Ontario. He encased kitchen matches in wax, so that they would survive the soil moisture and downpours. He had a rifle and ammunition to ward off the opportunists.

One evening, Dieter came up to my room and asked if he could use the phone. "Sure." He placed a call to Hans, the manager of his father's felt facility in Toronto. Then ensued a lengthy explanation to Hans of the plans to bury all the survival equipment and the cross-country trip to escape the atomic onslaught. "*Ja. Ja. Ja, Hans. Ja.*" Finally Dieter rang off, and I asked him how Hans had responded to his grand scheme. "Hans told me '**Dieter, if you survive, then *millions* will survive!**'"

Several weeks later, on a Friday evening, Dieter set out from New Haven in his VW on a dry run to Ontario. His car was filled with the aforementioned glass jars of survival staples. While proceeding Northwards on Route 8 in Seymour (Connecticut), Dieter missed the freeway exit. He changed directions at the next exit, but while exiting the correct ramp Southbound, he somehow hit the concrete dividing barrier between the highway and the exit. The VW overturned. All the jars broke, and the interior of the Bug took on the appearance of the inside of a cloud.

Dieter straight away recovered from the disaster and formulated a plan. I was to rent a U-Haul trailer, load up the crumpled Bug, drive to Port Newark where he had arranged to ship the automobile back to Braunshweig for repair. We implemented the plan, sure enough. But by the time we got onto the New Jersey Turnpike, a second disaster seemed imminent: the fog became so thick that one could discern only one or two stripes of the lane markers ahead of our tow car.

Of course, the Soviet missiles never arrived. And the VW Bug never returned to the US. Dieter eventually heard that after the repair, the vehicle had been sold to an elderly lady in Braunschweig. That happened to be Frau Genscher, the mother of Gesina, Dieter's childhood sweetheart. "No Damage History" was probably not included on the window sales sticker.

I spent my senior year at Yale in the Scholar of the House Program. So did Dick Morcroft. We were to spend the year researching and writing a thesis-length study on a subject of our choosing. We would meet with the other six Scholars once a week to enjoy a glass of sherry and dinner while listening to one of the group report on the progress he was making in the effort. Dick wrote about the Mexican presidential election campaign; I wrote about the aftermath of Juan Peron's disastrous rule of Argentina; Joe Lieberman, the future US Senator from Connecticut, wrote about Boss Bailey. A most rewarding experience. Although I must admit to some procrastination in the autumn months due to the exceptionally favorable sailing conditions on Long Island Sound.

Dieter had the sense to switch his major from Physics and Chemistry to German Literature. He wrote a small thesis that pleased Mr. Demitz, the head of the Department. Chas had graduated a year early, in 1963, and applied to Harvard Law School. Dick Morcroft and I applied to Yale Law School. Dieter, who married Katherine Whalley from Kingston, Ontario in the spring of 1964, applied to the Law School at Queen's University in Kingston. All applications were accepted, and we went our various ways.

I married Sue Tracy in June 1963, as planned. We lived out my Senior year in an apartment block in New Haven, Madison Towers. We then looked for a house, and subsequently purchased a waterfront property in Guilford, on the Harbor at Sachem's Head. I was able to moor my 26-foot sloop just at the head of that harbor.

My career as a law student lasted only four days. If you will recall Professor Kingsfield in the series *The Paper Chase*, you will get the flavor: sheer terror. Contracts Professor Lipson pulled the same tactic: when a student (and fortunately it was not I) entered the lecture hall several minutes late, Lipson halted the instruction mid-sentence, allowed the tardy example to take his seat, then finished the remainder of his sentence to a chorus of quiet snickers. Guido Calabresi taught torts. He instinctively knew that you didn't know the answer to his devilish questions, even before you opened your mouth.

I immediately formulated Plan B: armed with my copy of Professor

Chris Tunnard's book on City Planning,[1] I marched down York Street to the Art and Architecture School. I asked for an interview with Mr. Arthur Roe, the head of the City Planning Department. I explained my predicament and asked to transfer to the City Planning Course. Based solely upon my ability to get into the Law School in the first place, he graciously granted my request. I spent the next two years earning a Master's Degree in City Planning (MCP, an abbreviation that had another unfortunate connotation).

When I entered City Planning School, I expected basically a course in macro-landscape design: building or rebuilding cities based upon rational design criteria taking into account transportation, commercial and residential requirements to achieve a more livable and human urban experience. What I soon discovered was a mish-mash of pseudo-scientific sociological clap-trap, largely based on Progressive dogma related to the redistribution of wealth in favor of those willing to contribute less than their fair share of effort in creating a viable working civil entity.

So, I gravitated to a more simplistic endeavor, namely trying to understand the distribution of the population over the landscape: statistical geography, if you will. I drew upon my attempts in the Scholar of the House program to understand the population patterns in Argentina that influenced the political process. Soon, this developed into a means of displaying "population potential" in a graphic form. This measure pretends to display the "likelihood" of finding a person on the landscape, presented in graphic form as a distribution of dots on a map of a specific study area. Figure 3 shows the distribution of population in the State of Connecticut based upon the Census of 1960. The computer programs required to generate these displays, in effect, sucked me directly into the technical profession of computer programming.

---

1 Christopher Tunnard, *Man Made America: Chaos or Control* (New Haven, Yale University Press, 1963).

Figure 3: Population potential graphic.

As a graduate student, I was able to take courses in related fields. This permitted me to morph into the Computer Science realm and study under Robert Rosen, a brilliant computer practician with expertise in the development of computer languages at the University of Michigan. As I learned the techniques of this new field, I became familiar with the staff at the Yale Computer Center, their practices, and their computing facilities. Soon it became apparent that computer programming would provide me a more exciting career path than the practice of City Planning. I applied for, and was accepted, as a programmer on the staff of the Yale Computer Center.

CHAPTER IV

COMPUTER NERD

My career in computer programming really started when I was preparing my study of Argentine presidential election results for the Scholar of the House Program in my senior year at Yale. Data aggregated by county consisted of population, gender, age, income levels, and so forth, for every county in every Argentine province. Trends were determined by applying correlation and regression techniques to these data. Not only did the data have to be arranged and punched onto the cards, but the "canned program" that analyzed the data had to be shown how that data was organized (by columns) and which factor to compare with which other factor.

After entering graduate school, I became interested in statistical geography, the study of the distribution of population over the landscape. Computer programming became a necessary skill to be able to present the data in a graphic form. I received excellent instruction in a course taught by Professor Robert Rosen of the Engineering Department. Bob was also an advisor to the staff of the Yale Computer Center and was very helpful to me when I began to work there in the fall of 1966.

A slight distraction arose when my Selective Service Board in Virginia notified me that I should report for a physical. I took with me papers that showed that I had undergone surgery for an osteochondroma, a benign tumor just above my right knee that had affected my walking. My classification came back as "1Y" which meant suitable for military service, but only in the event of a declared war or national emergency, which Vietnam was not.

The Yale Computer Center ("YCC") already had a reasonably sophisticated IBM computer suite when I started. But, inexorably, advances in speed and capabilities were fast rendering the system inadequate. The University decided to combine the developments of two new IBM System 360 computers, one for YCC, and the other for Administrative Data Systems, the group that handled the University's budgeting, accounting, and payroll functions. The YCC staff of approximately fifteen set about designing a software system that could be used on both computer systems, allowing each to be utilized in the "time sharing mode", meaning that multiple users could be working simultaneously through typewriter like terminals and sharing the various computer resources such as data storage and printers without impeding other users.

My first job was to create the software changes to allow the incorporation of a line plotter into the hardware system. A 30-inch wide Calcomp Plotter used pen and ink to draw pictures on white paper. The device was employed, for instance, by Professor Harvey Boutwell of the Engineering School. He developed a program to design the overhead green directional signs for the Interstate Highway System, then in its infancy. Figure 4 shows the actual signs he used in developing and testing his program. They are still in place today on Interstate Route 395 in Connecticut, North of Putnam.

Figure 4: Interstate Highway signage.

My own efforts were then directed towards the incorporation of the various peripheral devices that operated sequentially (card reader, card punch, printer and line plotter) such that queues were established and managed behind the scenes in a process referred to as "spooling". If you, as a user, wanted a printed copy of the results of running your own computer program, you would issue a "PRINT" command on your terminal and provide the name of the dataset you wished to be printed. Seamlessly, the command would be placed in the printer queue and, in its turn, the file would be printed out and stacked for you to pick up at a later time.

System programs, such as those used in the spooling process, had to be written in the basic instruction set provided by the manufacturer of the machine, in this case IBM. So we all had to learn a brand new computer language before we could even start. Then, in addition to the normal process of creating a program and debugging it through multiple iterations, we also had to contend with the annoying fact that the underlying system provided by IBM was itself replete with its own errors. Discovering, documenting, and correcting these errors took time and effort and added considerably to the expense of system development.

Yale's new system was called "CYTOS", an acronym for Conversational Yale Terminal Operating System. It allowed students and faculty to write their own programs online, instead of the traditional "batch" method of submitting card decks for sequential processing. A set of terminal "commands" provided the various abilities to create, edit, run, and debug the individual user programs. Each command (e.g., PRINT or EDIT) represented a complicated system program, written in machine language that had to operate error-free. Many months and much effort went into perfecting CYTOS, but the final result exceeded most expectations.

The staff at the Yale Computer Center was a very cohesive group; we all got along with each other famously. My lesson to remember from this experience is that good leadership, when coupled with talented and enthusiastic personnel can produce marvelous results. Many from this team I still count as close friends.[1]

Systems such as CYTOS lasted only a short while, due to the arrival of smaller and more powerful computers that allowed each user his own dedicated system. These eventually morphed into the personal desktop devices still in common use today. Yale, in the meantime, was undergoing financial strain and one fallout was the dramatic downsizing of the Computer Center staff. Including Yours Truly.

IBM developed one of these smaller systems, the 1130. It ran in the batch mode, like the older, bigger systems. My thought was to create CYTOS on the 1130 system so that an engineer, say, could sit down at the system control typewriter and use the machine in a conversational mode, the same as on the IBM 360 at Yale. So I created Eleven Thirty, Incorporated, consisting of a purchased IBM 1130 computer with printer and card reader/punch, a small office in Guilford, Connecticut and myself as President, Programmer, and Dish Washer.

After about a year of feverish programming, in yet another unique machine language I had to learn from scratch, I had a viable enough package that I thought might be marketable. I attended a conference of 1130 System users in Kansas City, which provided me a platform to tout the features of my CYTOS package. Bud Blackney approached me after the lecture and expressed high interest in the product. Bud was one of three partners of DNA Systems, an offshoot created by three Dow Chemical employees in Midland, Michigan. DNA had developed their own programs for the 1130 and 1800 systems sold by IBM. They had a customer list and thought that CYTOS would add some interest to their basket of products.

New and faster computers were on the drawing boards, and some could be programmed to "emulate" an older machine such as the 1130. DNA was involved in one of these projects. The added capabilities of

1 Greydon Freeman, Rest in Peace.

these newer computers allowed us to consider the creation of a small time-sharing capability, similar to the one developed at Yale. I worked several more years on this augmentation, and DNA was able to market the new CYTOS II as well. DNA produced their own time-sharing system that used the first CYTOS. In as much as this created a slight conflict of interest for Eleven Thirty, Inc., I decided to sell the rights to CYTOS to DNA and move on to other projects.

After eight or so years of programming computers, I began to feel that writing one more program, no matter its purpose, became pretty much the same as writing the previous program. The skill I had learned I knew would always be valuable, and something I could fall back on if need be. In fact, several years later I was able to draw upon these talents to create a set of accounting programs for a new business that I had helped found, Perma Treat. Today, I still use many of these programs for my own personal book-keeping.

CHAPTER V
SACHEM FUND

My wife and I settled into our shore-line cottage in Guilford, Connecticut in the fall of 1964. The structure of 1920's vintage required considerable renovation, but we were happy with the results. For a while.

Eventually, we found that the frame house on the one-half acre of land just did not provide the privacy that we sought. We commissioned Sydney Miller, an architect from New Haven, to design a new contemporary house for us based upon the design of his own home; that is to say, four wings arranged around a central courtyard. The old house was torn down (we moved to a rental for the winter) just after the 1968 General Election. The new house was not completed until late 1970, though we moved into the shell in the summer of 1969.

The design was a single story with a flat roof and large sliding glass windows. It displeased our neighbors to the East because it stuck out farther towards the water than the original house, and therefore blocked their view of the sunsets in the summer. Sachem's Head is an association chartered by the State of Connecticut, similar to Fenwick in Old Saybrook, where Katherine Hepburn used to live. Sachem's Head is populated primarily with professional folk, some of them being of the attitude that their status and longevity in the community gave them special privileges. Our neighbor was one of these. Nonetheless, we persevered, and the house still stands.

We found a golden retriever and named him after my Yale roommate, Dieter, because he slept with his eyes open (and also couldn't hold his water for long stretches). Of course we had to rename him, so as not to offend one of our first visitors. "Puppy" then became our best friend. He distinguished himself by often picking up three tennis balls in his mouth. Once he actually picked up four. Puppy would also chase the flashlight beam as it ascended the wall, crossed the ceiling, and descended on the other side, never quite to be caught. I would ride my bicycle through the suburban streets at full speed; Puppy would never fail to keep up. After thirteen wonderful years, that saddest day inevitably arrived where we had to put him down. (Writer's tears.)

Having been released by the Computer Center, I had considerable time on my hands to oversee the construction of this new abode. A good thing: unless you are there every day, errors are made, which left for very long, cannot be corrected without incurring considerable extra expense. One day, to my amazement, I discovered that the garage, which was the fourth side around our courtyard, was half a course of concrete block off the levels of the other three sides.

And of course the general contractor promised that the plumber or the electrician would be there the very next day . . . yeah. Constant haranguing became part of the process.

The old garage still stood in the corner of the lot and was used to store equipment and such during the building process. I also used it as a shop, having time to build a new dining room table for our new dining hall. I modeled the table on one I had seen in an opera we attended in Munich: *Macbeth* (an Englishman's story about a Dane, sung in Germany in Italian by an American). In the second Scene of Act I, the King presides at his feast: a long narrow table with benches on either side. In my version, two 10-foot long and 15-inch wide and 3-inch thick pieces of maple are supported at each end by a solid square column of oak. Once finished, it took considerable effort for me to move it, single-handedly, around through the courtyard and into the new dining room. Homage is due to my instructor from Fenn School, Charles Ward.

We also made much use of our 26-foot sloop, the UKIYO. UKIYO is derived from Japanese and means, as I recall, "pleasures of the floating world", or some such. She was designed by Danny Knott and built at the Chester A. Crosby boat yard in Osterville, Massachusetts, close to where my family spent their summers. It was a graduation present to me from my father. Four more of the Curlew class were built by Crosby, one of which my father purchased (the "Cornflower").

Figure 5: Tim's table (with one bench).

So I would keep the boat at Crosby's each winter, sail to Connecticut each spring, then return each autumn in late October. The non-stop trip usually took about 30 hours, and had to be planned around favorable wind and tide patterns. Sue and I sailed to Nantucket and back during our honeymoon. We took other longer trips, venturing as far North as Tenants Harbor in Maine and as far Southwest as Lower New York City. We also once circumnavigated Cape Cod.

My wife and I now had more time also to consider new endeavors. We formed a small private foundation, the Sachem Fund, with the intention of investing in innovative solutions to problems that seemed to plague our society. We tackled problems of poverty, race and environmental despoliation that were overwhelming the country; we favored small, un-bureaucratic organizations that could efficiently apply the modest contributions we were able to make. Some of the projects, like the first Hospice in Branford, Connecticut, were successful; others fell short of our hopes. Still being of the Liberal persuasion at that age in our lives, I believe we may have overlooked some fundamental attributes of human nature that would have precluded success in any case.

Still involved tangentially with Yale University, we were introduced to Ernie Osborne who worked in the Office of Development. Ernie and Betty Osborne lived in New Haven and shared an enthusiasm for positive thinking. Sue and I were able to convince Ernie to become president of our Sachem Fund and broaden the reach of our efforts. After several years, adversity claimed the Osborne family: Betty's brother Warren was involved with the Black Panther movement in New Haven and was jailed after being implicated in the murder of the alleged stool pigeon Sams. Not long thereafter, their son (also named Warren) contracted cancer, which quickly claimed his life. Maybe you can imagine their grief.

One of the very first projects considered by the Sachem Fund was a proposal to resurrect the Poughkeepsie Bridge, a landmark railroad structure across the Hudson River owned by the New Haven Railroad. The New Haven had been consumed in the creation of the Penn Central from the amalgamation of the Pennsylvania Railroad with the New York Central. The track from New Haven, over this magnificent bridge, to Maybrook Yard had been abandoned as superfluous. One evening, totally by chance, Sue and I attended a lecture at the Guilford chapter of League of Women Voters. The speaker was a Mr. David Fink, one of the newly installed managers on the Penn Central, and his subject was the Poughkeepsie Bridge and the rationalization of the rail system in New England.

We quickly enlisted Mr. Fink's assistance to promote our scheme. He had several conversations with representatives of the Connecticut Department of Transportation, but the upshot was that, even with some state subsidy, no viable use could be made of the old route, and that therefore the Poughkeepsie Bridge would remain nothing more than a glorious reminder of the bygone days of railroading in New England.

Sachem Fund struggled on for several more years, but without the dynamism of Ernie Osborne's leadership. He departed to head the Council of Foundations, which was a much more important organization in the scheme of things in the world of charity. Eventually, the corpus of the trust was distributed to several large organizations involved on the other side of the spectrum of ideas, such as the Heritage Foundation.

CHAPTER VI

PERMA TREAT

Some months after the lecture at the League of Women Voters, I got a telephone call from Dave Fink. He said that he and an associate of his from the Guilford Wetlands Commission had been working on a plan to build and operate a sawmill and pressure treating plant in Durham, Connecticut, just North of Guilford. He asked if I had any interest and, hearing "yes", proposed that he and Ned Bartlett come down to chat about it. Ned was the son of Edwin Bartlett, who owned a sawmill in North Guilford and who also served as First Selectman for the Town of Guilford.

We met, discussed the viability of the project, and agreed to go forward. We called for assistance from my attorney in Pittsburgh, who suggested hiring Price Waterhouse to prepare a proper business plan. By July of 1977 we had formed a corporation, set our eyes on a piece of land in Durham, ordered the turnkey creosote treating equipment and sawmill, achieved the requisite zoning permissions, and set in place the financing.

The building foundations were timely completed. However, the retort for the pressure treating process was delayed in delivery from Mississippi. Finally, on Christmas Day in 1977, the special movement over Conrail was to arrive in Springfield, Massachusetts. Dave Fink and I drove up to Russell, Massachusetts to observe the train descending the mountain. From our perch alongside US Route 20, I could see that the door of the retort was hinged on the wrong side! Dave was apoplectic. He called Tom Lippencott, the purveyor from Wilmington, North Carolina and threatened a reign of terror should he not correct the defect and install the equipment in a timely manner.

Tom Lippencott hastened North with a welder and helper in tow. It took them several days in (for them) quite inclement weather, to reverse the door hinges from one side to the other. Tom was frugal, we learned. He shared a room with the welder at the Holiday Inn in Meriden. One evening he returned to the room to find the welder "entertaining" a lady. When he showed up the next morning at our office he asked to use the phone. I heard him talking to his headquarters about the incident: "I told him I wasn't runnin' no who' house here!" Tom was especially sensitive to breaches of ethics and morality. He wore a lapel pin that featured the words "Try God". My wife, a talented jeweler in gold, fabricated pins for us that proclaimed "Try Perma Treat".

Well, in spite of Global Warming, the winter 1977–78 was one of the worst for Connecticut in many years. The retort was placed on its cradle in the specially designed building which still lacked a roof. Then it snowed feet. Then the snow all melted. Then the melted water in the containment levy, 15 inches deep, froze solid. The boiler didn't work, so hot water could not be sent through pipes to melt the ice. Finally, our genius electrician Tom Caputo touched the two magical wires together and, WHOOSH! The boiler ignited and saved the day. He went back to his truck, pulled out a bottle of Canadian Club, and celebrated the success with a happy Dave.

Our first production of railroad ties emerged on Valentine's Day, 1978. They were inspected and accepted by Amtrak. Dave rushed down to Philadelphia to pick up the check. We also earned save-the-bacon money by using our front-end loader to plow out Conrail's New Haven freight yards from the next blizzard. Traffic was banned from travel on all Connecticut highways. When we returned, bleary-eyed, in the dawn hours, we were subjected to severe and unrelenting uxorial wrath.

Perma Treat was located in Durham on a piece of farmland purchased from Mr. Fitzgerald. We found it whilst hi-railing up the old Air Line Route from New Haven through Middletown. Because of a stream, it was landlocked from an adjacent state highway, Route 163. The price for the piece of land was, therefore, quite reasonable. However, permits were rapidly granted from the Department of Environmental protection to install an eight foot diameter culvert to allow passage over the stream, thanks to Dave's previous associations with Department of Environmental Protection ("DEP") while employed with the Tomasso Company. When Mr. Fitzgerald saw us fording the brook the next week, he was livid.

The plan was to create an industrial park, "Air Line Park", wherein Perma Treat would build its plant on the back 20 acres, and the remainder of the land would be subdivided into six more lots for smaller enterprises, each accessible not only by a new road, but also by a railroad spur that we would build connecting the park to the Air Line. Sue was anxious to participate in the project and offered to finance the remaining development. We received all the requisite permits, built the road, a pond and a railroad spur, all the while tending to our new fledgling business that struggled to ramp up production to a profitable level.

Perma Treat thrived thereafter, but there was scant interest in the remaining lots from prospective buyers. My wife became increasingly impatient and incensed at the lack of real-estate demand. To placate her, Dave offered for Perma Treat to repurchase her interest for whatever she had invested in it. She agreed, grudgingly, but the atmosphere thereafter was poisoned forever. Lesson of Life: do not allow loved ones or relatives to co-invest in private ventures. DO NOT.

Other entrepreneurial opportunities came my way in roughly the same timeframe as the creation of Perma Treat. DNA and I both invested in a computer company called Vertical Systems that had connections to yet another computer manufacturer of IBM 1130 clones. The plan was to set up a subsidiary in Saudi Arabia using the connections of the VSI President, Jack Merry. What a fiasco! Any such venture requires a Saudi royal for a partner, who, for 50 percent of the stock, does nothing but lend his name; then there are the outrageous costs of doing anything in a country so foreign and so far away; finally, the straw that broke the camel's back (haha!) was the absconding of about $50,000 by the local manager, who deftly escaped back to his Pakistani homeland. Lesson of Life: the grass on the other side of the fence might actually be **sand** . . . or **quicksand**.

And then there was the Insulating Shade Company. Having built the aforementioned house in Guilford, my wife and I became interested in the possibility of solar heating. We contracted with Sunworks, a local solar provider, to install 20 panels on the flat roof of our garage. The system provided all of our hot water, and in addition, about 40 percent of the annual house heating energy (backed up by an oil furnace). Tom Hopper was an engineer who helped design the system for Sunworks.

Chatting with Tom one day, he spun a description of an invention he was working on: an insulating window shade that rolled up onto a dowel at the top of the window. Would I possibly be interested in investing in a company that would manufacture and sell such a device? Of course, being in the middle of an energy crisis made "yes" an easy answer. Roll out the lawyers for new agreements, find a place, and all the other startup whirlwinds.

The device envisaged by Tom consisted of an outer (room-side) layer of vinyl and four inner layers of metalized Mylar™. The end of these layers was attached to a fixed rod, and the other ends attached to the roller, such that when fully extended, the five parallel layers of material formed four airspaces. The layers were to be forced apart from one another about one-half inch by strips of Mylar™ curved by a heat process into a slight arc. The combination of the airspaces and the reflectivity of the Mylar™ is what created the insulating property. When measured by a laboratory in Lancaster, Pennsylvania, the prototype achieved a value of R-13, quite impressive.

But now Tom also had to invent and build the machine that would produce this window shade. And another machine that would create the Mylar™ arcs. And a sprocket for one end of the roller that would allow the shade to be deployed using a beaded chain. And the computer program that would control the machinery. Gus Carlson, Tom's mechanical design assistant, and I began to have misgivings about how long it was going to take before getting into production. Meanwhile, tragedy struck: first, Tommy Magness, a great young kid, and son of the company's secretary Pat Magness, was killed in an automobile accident. Next, fire consumed one half of the old manufacturing building in which our company was located. We lost nothing, but the Fire Marshall decided to condemn the whole building, so everything came to a grinding halt while we found another venue.

Tom, non-plussed, continued to tinker and perfect his new machines, almost oblivious to the business implications of our situation. Finally, at a Board meeting held to chart a new course, a strike of lightning and a loud clap of thunder within yards of our meeting, brought things to a climax: "Enough!" I yelled, "that's it!" To make a long story short, we removed Tom Hopper from the company, built a new manufacturing plant at Air Line Park in Durham, redesigned (and received a new patent on) a new shade that was far simpler to manufacture, and revitalized our marketing efforts. Lesson of Life: Beware the Inventor—he can't stop inventing.

Nonetheless, our efforts and good fortunes were short-lived. It turned out that the plasticizer in the outer vinyl sheet leached and caused discoloration of the shiny Mylar™ layers. Not only was the product's appearance damaged, but the R-value of the device was compromised to the point we could no longer warrant its efficacy. Back to the lawyers, who brought a successful lawsuit against the manufacturers of the vinyl for failing to warn us of these side effects. Compensation from the lawsuit meant that our last year in business was our only profitable year. How ironic.

Some years later, Dick Kelso, a classmate from the Hill School in Virginia, introduced me to another entrepreneurial opportunity. He worked for Jim Wheat's investment firm, which had undertaken to organize investors for a newly created company called Geostar. The company was founded by Jerry O'Neill, a Professor of Physics at Princeton University. O'Neill had invented and patented a system to determine the geographical position of a transmitter by means of triangulating radio signals through transponders attached to geo-stationary satellites in low Earth orbit. One of the Board Members of Geostar was Luis Alvarez, the scientist who had developed the theory that the extinction of the dinosaurs was caused by the catastrophic encounter of an asteroid with the Yucatan Peninsula in Mexico.

By this time we had already been in the railroad business for several years. My interest in Geostar stemmed from the possibility of being able to determine the precise location of trains on our system, independent of the traditional block control systems traditionally employed. So I made a sizeable investment in Geostar on the condition that our subsidiary, "Railstar", could develop and market the rights to the technology for railroads and other "fixed route transportation systems."

Our own software development to perfect this technology was proceeding on schedule, but Geostar itself ran into difficulties. They needed two different types of transponders. The simpler of the two merely accepted signals from the ground radios and passed them on to Geostar's computer for analysis and determination of position. The more complicated version performed the same function, but in addition sent the outbound signal to query the ground radio, as well as returning the unit's geographical position after the analysis. Geostar had contracted with the French to place the simpler version on an Arianne rocket to be launched from French Guiana. The launch was successful and the Geostar unit performed as expected.

The more complicated unit, however, due to launch delays and other internal Geostar problems, never made it into orbit. In addition, Professor O'Neill was diagnosed with leukemia and was essentially sidelined from the corporate efforts and problems for the remainder of his unfortunately short lifespan. Railstar was left holding a large developmental bag. Efforts to replace the Geostar technology with the newly available GPS receivers proved ineffectual due to transmission delays inherent in the relay through the satellite transponder. We folded our tent and placed the proprietary developments on ice.

CHAPTER VII

RAILROADS

While toiling in Durham producing railroad ties, our corporate minds naturally gravitated into imaginations of how to grow and expand our business. My partner Dave Fink came from a family of railroaders: his father was superintendent on the Pennsylvania Railroad in charge of the commuter operations in Philadelphia. Dave himself had worked on the Pennsylvania Railroad and its merged remnant, the hapless Penn Central. After the Penn Central bankruptcy, he worked for Tomasso, the Connecticut construction materials company: Dave was in charge of its subsidiary, a short-line railroad that carried crushed rock from a quarry in North Branford to a barge loading facility on Long Island Sound. Tomasso also had their own fleet of hopper cars to serve their other quarries in Southern New England, situated on the major railroads.

Dave imagined that we could take advantage of the lucrative per diem rates on various types of freight cars if we could only get a hold of a small short-line railroad to establish its bona-fide railroad ownership. Depending upon age and quality, these "free-runner" cars could make money for the owning railroad, whether loaded or empty, so long as they were located "abroad". So we investigated the availability of such an entity and before long, got wind of the Grafton and Upton, a line in Central Massachusetts with one or two customers, on ten miles of track.

The Grafton and Upton was, in fact, owned by one of those customers.

In turn, that company was owned by Rockwell International. Rockwell was, indeed, interested in divesting itself of the railroad to simplify its regulatory exposure. We obtained the financial metrics (carloads, revenues, expenses and so forth) and set out to make an offer to purchase. Dave and I travelled to the Pittsburgh headquarters of Rockwell International to make our pitch. Because the railroad in its then present financial state was basically a losing proposition, we offered to take it off their hands if they would *pay us* $85,000. They showed us politely to the door, thank you. (Undoubtedly, there were complex accounting issues such as depreciation recapture on Rockwell's books that we just had no knowledge of.) Nice try.

Not long discouraged by our initial failure, we determined that there might be even greater advantages to owning and operating a full-sized railroad property. Our Pittsburgh attorney learned that the Pittsburgh and Lake Erie Railroad ("P&LE") was soon to be up for sale. The P&LE hauled coal and steel, primarily. Their physical plant was in good condition and included some valuable real estate assets near downtown Pittsburgh. We called on our friends at Dillon Reed to evaluate the property (actually, Dave had to more or less teach them how to evaluate a railroad) so that we could make a sensible bid. Hank Sharp, the president of the P&LE, was putting together a group that also wanted to purchase the property. The bidding process ran its course, the other group won the bid, but unfortunately they left $15,000,000 on the table! Their profligacy assured that the railroad would not long survive: after several years, the P&LE was absorbed into CSX, one of the three remaining Eastern Railroad giants.

Next we looked at the Illinois Central Gulf Railroad ("ICG"), owned by the IC Industries conglomerate. The ICG basically was a North–South operation between Chicago, St. Louis and New Orleans. Grain was a major component of its commodity mix, so it received considerable competition from the Mississippi barge traffic. In any case, the asking price was what we considered to be exorbitant and, save for an amusing ride on Billy Johnson's yacht from Essex across Long Island Sound, we took home nothing for our efforts. The ICG is now part of Canadian National.

Neither Dave nor I discouraged easily. Our next foray involved railroads closer to home. At one point in his career, Dave Fink had worked for Ashland Oil, a Kentucky oil refiner. By 1980, Ashland Oil was proud owner of the US Filter Company, which in turn was owner of the Maine Central Railway. Filter's Chairman Ray Rich had visions of merging the Maine Central with the Boston and Maine Railroad. This combination had been the long-term dream of Buck Dumaine, the New Hampshire industrialist who oversaw Amoskeag Mills.

The Boston and Maine had been in bankruptcy for some time. We visited Alan Dustin, its president, and explained that we might be interested in purchasing the railroad out of bankruptcy. He arranged a hi-rail trip (Suburban automobile outfitted with rail wheels) from Lowell up to Portland, Maine, where it met the Maine Central Railway. We met John Gerrity, president of the Maine Central, who escorted us over the few miles of the Portland Terminal Railroad, a 50–50 joint venture between B&M and MEC. On our departure, John waved us off with a cheery "Hope to see you again some day!" (Little did he suspect. . . .) Dustin arranged for us to meet with the two trustees, and we furthered our proposal, but indicated that a purchase offer would be conditioned upon our first being able to secure the Maine Central. The two railroads belonged together, but history had shown that apart, they tended to harm each other by diverting traffic to other connections.

Since Dave had worked at Ashland, he knew Orin Atkins, Ashland's Chairman. One phone call to Atkins from Dave was sufficient to determine that Orin Atkins was not in favor of Mr. Rich's attempts to expand the railroad empire. In fact Orin Atkins wanted to extract his companies from such regulated businesses altogether. Atkins was just about to leave for the Middle East, but we were able to hastily arrange a meeting in the departure lounge at Kennedy Airport prior to his flight. Dave and I hopped in my little single-engine Piper Tomahawk and flew straight away from New Haven to JFK for the meeting. It took less than an hour for all to agree on a purchase and sale, and a price of $15,000,000.

The lawyers put together the paperwork and the signatures were sealed upon Mr. Atkins' return. Ray Rich was beside himself. Atkins had informed him that if he failed to have the US Filter Board of Directors ratify this deal immediately, he, Ray Rich would be summarily removed from all positions at US Filter by vote of the majority stockholder, Ashland Oil. Ray Rich summoned Dave and me to his palatial office high up in the Pan Am building over Grand Central Station in New York. He offered to personally buy the Maine Central Railroad from us for a price of four million dollars over the price we had negotiated. We said "NO", of course, smiled, and took our leave.

The Boston and Maine Railroad was not quite so easy to procure. It had languished in bankruptcy for some years: every law firm in Boston represented some creditor or debtor, and the *ching-ching-ching* of the cash register made them reluctant to bring the process to a conclusion. Federal Bankruptcy Judge Frank Murray was in no particular hurry either. Once, during oral argument, he was caught napping on the bench. Other groups were interested in the B&M, but our offer of $24.5 million was sufficient to persuade the two trustees, Messrs. Robert Meserve and Ben Lacy, to press for a settlement and release the railroad back into the real world. For not only would the extra traffic generated by the combination of the B&M and the MEC create healthier revenues for both, but the synergies to be achieved from reducing managerial duplicate efforts would add even more to the bottom line. Finally, the reorganization was approved at the end of June 1983.

From 1981 to 1983, then, Maine Central was our only railroad.

I assumed the positions of Chairman and Chief Executive officer of our holding company, Guilford Transportation Industries (named, of course after the Connecticut town that was the crucible of our partnership). Dave Fink became its president. Spencer Miller remained Chairman of the Maine Central. However, it was readily apparent that he would not willingly abandon "old ways" and permit us to slim down the ungainly managerial apparatus that he had put in place over the years. In due course, Mr. Miller was convinced to retire. Dave became MEC Chairman and John Gerrity remained as president.

The property was fraught with inefficiencies. There were old branch lines that were maintained, even though the cost of maintenance could never be recouped from the revenues generated from the paltry amount of traffic on each line. The ballast used under the track was washed river gravel, which made the roadbed quite unstable and susceptible to frequent washouts and repairs. We switched immediately to crushed granite, each piece having sharp edges that could readily interlock with its neighbors. Track maintenance gangs would travel up and down on hand carts instead of using modern pick-up trucks to reach their work stations. Dave could never get a straight answer as to how many employees populated the Main Office Building in Portland. So one day he set off the fire alarm, having pre-stationed someone at each doorway to count the people evacuating the building. Yes, they counted way more people than expected!

While busy settling into the Maine Central, we also turned our attention to yet a third railroad, the Delaware and Hudson ("D&H"). The D&H connected with the B&M at Mechanicsville, New York, and from there ran all the way West to Buffalo, North to Montreal, and South (via trackage rights) to Potomac Yard in Alexandria, Virginia. The D&H was a subsidiary of the Norfolk and Western Railway ("N&W"). It was a poor cousin received years earlier in a transaction with the Pennsylvania Railroad. The N&W was anxious to rid itself of this millstone, as it did nothing to add to their bottom line. One day while driving through Connecticut, I heard Mr. John Fishwick (N&W Chief Executive Officer) being interviewed on the radio. Asked what the D&H was worth, he responded "$250,000". To us, however, an extension to the West would not only allow us to carry our traffic further, but combining it with the other two railroads would create yet more synergies.

So we flew to Norfolk to chat with Robert Claytor, president of the N&W, about a purchase. "What do you think you'd be willing to pay for the D&H?" he asked. I piped up immediately, "Well, *$250,000;* I heard Mr. Fishwick say that was what the D&H was worth!" When Mr. Claytor regained his composure, he came back with "Do you think you could possibly consider $500,000? Just for appearance sake?" We had a deal. Later, we discovered that the President's office at the D&H contained a small collection of art, worth more, in aggregate, as I remember, than the purchase price of the entire railroad. We gifted one of these paintings to Mr. Claytor as a thank-you. What the story doesn't reveal is the large amount of debt on the D&H books that we would have to assume. That, and the deferred maintenance on the track structure, made the real cost of the acquisition much higher.

Once these three deals had been struck, we needed to obtain approval from the Interstate Commerce Commission ("ICC"). Their charge was to make sure that mergers did not reduce competition or lead to monopoly strength. Shippers were allowed to ask for special conditions if they were to be adversely affected. Of course, competing railroads could be counted on to complain that a merger such as ours would cost them in reduced traffic and revenues. In our case, Canadian National Railway and Canadian Pacific squealed the loudest, but in reality, the main reason they complained was because the increased competition would cause them to reduce their rates, thus benefitting the shippers. The ICC rightly ignored their whines. Once the ICC approved, our last hurdle was waiting for Judge Murray to approve the B&M reorganization, which seemingly took forever.

Scrambling the eggs to create one viable operating entity was not so easy as one might think. Each of the three railroads was a little empire unto itself. Then, within each, the various departments were little bastions of power and ego. We had to choose the best talent for each consolidated function. Often, the best answer was "None of the three." The shining exception was Sydney Culliford, head of the Transportation Department on the Boston & Maine. He was, and remains, a man of high character, integrity, enthusiasm and talent. Sydney just retired in 2014. All the others are long gone and forgotten. Dave Fink was able to replace the weakest by bringing in talent from the Conrail reorganization: Charlie McKenna, Glen Hartsoe and Walter Riscorla. He forged a new team, bit by bit, that could ignore the old rivalries and adversarial

Photo © Louise Mellon

Figure 6: Guilford train on the Nicholson Viaduct in Pennsylvania.

policies, because they were not part of them. A working management was functioning well by the end of 1985.

Soon we were setting our focus on even more distant goals. The US Government, owner of the Conrail behemoth, was anxious to get out of the railroad business, having poured billions into the salvation of railroading in the Northeast. Both CSX and Norfolk Southern were interested purchasers. But selling Conrail to just one of the two, without compensating adjustments, would have created an unhealthy competitive situation and certain damage to the one who lost out. We were able to convince Norfolk Southern that their bid would only be successful if, in turn, they would agree to divest enough of Conrail to a partner, such as us, so as to avoid this dilemma. We proposed that routes Westward from Buffalo to St. Louis and Chicago would be an appropriate solution. They tentatively agreed, but the routes they were willing to give up were in such rag-tag condition that both we and the Department of Justice determined that the "solution" was basically a sham. Better routes were offered. The US Senate approved the concept, but Mr. Dingle (D-MI) was able to prevent the House of Representatives from going along. Labor's fear that the loss of so many jobs would decimate their unions was the factor that essentially scotched the deal.

At the same time, our six-year long labor contracts were corning up for re-negotiation. Labor saw this coincidence as a means of queering the entire Conrail deal. The Brotherhood of Maintenance of Way Employees ("BMWE", those guys that maintain the tracks) proposed a wage hike that was on the verge of Draconian. They figured that if we were so intent on participating in Conrail that we should just roll over and agree. And we did come partway, and also offered some compensating benefits. But the last additional 15 cents per hour was just too bitter a pill to swallow. If we paid it to them, we would have to give the same extra amount to all those represented by the other unions.

Great pressure was brought to bear by some of our board members to accept the deal and just figure out later how to pay for it. I remember meeting in a Philadelphia hotel where our Human Resources folks were talking to the union representatives. I was not feeling well that day, and when urged at the last minute to seal the deal, I rose up from my "sick bed" and cried "No, Goddammit!" Hours later, the representative of the National Mediation Board accompanied the BMWE Chairman to the microphone to announce that the failed negotiations had led to a strike.

So the Conrail deal fell by the wayside, to be concluded some years later. Our acquisitions were at an end. We faced a new challenge that would change our company forever. It would also change the entire rail industry.

CHAPTER VIII
THE STRIKES

The railroad and airline industries are subject to a different set of labor laws than are all other industries in the United States. The Railway Labor Act was passed in 1926 as a result of post-WWI labor disputes that threatened to harm the growing economy. In essence, the law is designed to make it very difficult for any party to bring matters to a point where interstate commerce is disrupted. It calls for a very rigid protocol with respect to how labor contracts are negotiated, implemented and thereafter changed. Once in place, a labor contract never ends: it can only be modified by agreement on changes by both management and labor. If agreement cannot be reached, elaborate procedures ensue to force the parties through mediation, and then if agreement still cannot be reached, by invocation of Emergency Boards that have the power to settle the dispute(s) and impose a new time limit before new proposals for change can be offered (usually three years).

The Maine Central strike ran this entire protocol before the strike was ended by the passage of the Emergency Board's recommended settlement by the US Congress. The normal practice was followed, whereby the management's last offer was used as a basis for this settlement. The underlying reason for the inability of the two sides to come to agreement lay in the implementation of railroad deregulation. As part of an effort in the late 1970s to shore up the gradually failing railroad industry, freight railroads were allowed much wider latitude in pricing their services. This permitted them to compete more effectively with the trucking and barge industries. But in all businesses, there are two sides of the ledger: revenues and costs. When revenues decreased in order to retain traffic, it put a further squeeze on profits because there was no ability or flexibility to modify the cost side of the business. A company that had to wait three years even before the start of a new round of contract bargaining might be weakened enough by that time that it would have to declare bankruptcy. And many railroads did so: the Erie, the Rock Island, the New Haven, and the Boston & Maine, to mention a few.

Guilford's three railroads were all suffering from this squeeze. In our view, if we did not break the vicious cycle of giving in to labor's every demand, then shortly there would be no more business to save. So ahead we plunged, having only the Florida East Coast as a template upon which to base our strategy of surviving what could become a very lengthy and costly and divisive struggle. As Dave Fink was fond of saying about these dark days, "We were too stupid to realize that we could actually lose. . . ." Other railroads "helped" us by trying to divert all our traffic. Customers complained about the disruption of service, not understanding that if the railroad failed, there would be no service anyway. Most hurt were those employees who felt they had to honor the picket line: union strike benefits lasted only so long, yet the car and house payments continued relentlessly.[1]

Most disappointing to me was the ostrich-like behavior of the US Congress. I was asked to come testify to the House Subcommittee on Commerce, Transportation, and Tourism, headed by New Jersey Congressman James Florio (D), about the obstinacy of our company in

1 Of course, the railroads' own economics were also in disarray. Some of our invoices were so old that we began to refer to them as Polish Payables; in other words, so old that even the Obligee had forgotten about them.

light of the most reasonable demands of the Brotherhood of Maintenance of Way Employees. I pointed out to the Chairman the absurdity of de-regulating the revenue side of railroad economics without corresponding relaxation of control of the cost side: railroads would have to be free to bargain their own contracts without being subject to oversight and second-guessing by the government. I pointed out that there were 16 unions on the Maine Central, 15 on the Boston and Maine, and 17 on the Delaware and Hudson. If the Chairman and his committee were going to oversee each and every bargaining conflict, they would be spending full time doing nothing but solving our labor disputes!

The Irony of Politics: some years later, Jim Florio ran for the Governorship of New Jersey, and won. He soon discovered that the tax revenues were insufficient to cover the profligate spending habits of the state government. He attempted to raise taxes instead of making an effort to pare down the expenses. At the next election, he lost his job.

The railroad, for its part, had to keep running as best it could. Managers became engineers and conductors. We scoured the landscape for railroad types who would come to work for us under severely strained conditions. Sydney Culliford found people in Ohio, Pennsylvania, Virginia, and as far away as Wyoming. I would fly out in my Aerostar and retrieve five at a time, bring them back for training and service.[2] Many only lasted a few days; others stuck it out hoping for eventual full time employment. We have only suffered three fatalities in thirty years of railroading, but two of those were during the strike. Unknown agents caused the derailing of a freight train in Cobelskill, New York. Another train idling in Ayer was set running with no-one aboard. Agile response by the dispatchers forced the train to run all the way to East Deerfield,

2 Replacement workers have been referred to as "scabs". Colin Pease, our Minister of Propaganda at Guilford, enjoyed pointing out that the Scab is the first phase in the healing process.

where it was allowd to slam into a string of empty freight cars to bring it to a halt. Luckily, not a soul was hurt.

Because of a short labor stoppage on the Boston & Maine before our stewardship, Sydney Culliford had become familiar with the efficacy of using a helicopter to carry crews to outlying points where the train had to be stopped because of the legal limitation on the hours of service. Prior to our strike, we had purchased a Jet Ranger helicopter, partially in anticipation of just such an eventuality. I was the pilot. Not only did replacing crews in short order have the effect of keeping the trains moving, but it also made for faster turnaround of the crews for their next trip, thus maximizing the availability of the limited pool of talent. Near the picket line at the entrance of the railroad's headquarters in North Billerica, someone had placed a crude painting on a folding chair. It showed a helicopter flying upside down, with the pilot (me) saying in a bubble, "Is this an emergency yet?" We have preserved that painting as a memento.

Figure 7: Jet Ranger N2JC, Guilford's secret weapon.

In frustration with the ungainly procedures of the Railway Act, we prepared a prototype labor agreement that we had every intention of issuing at the next available opportunity. This contract eschewed all seniority: employment was to be based solely on fitness and ability. Furthermore, the contract would be not with the union, but with the employee *per se*. There would be no class or craft, only the designation of "Railroader". And all work rules would be eliminated. Employees would be expected to work eight hours a day for eight hours pay, and they could be assigned to whatever type of work for which they were deemed fit, based solely on the judgment of management. As it turned out, we never had to present this proposed contract because the settlement imposed by Congress and the National Mediation Board relieved us of all the work rules anyway, and allowed us to assign employees to work outside their traditional craft for up to 50 percent of their time at work.

Some of the most valuable increase in productivity derived from the elimination of the differentiation between "road service" and "yard service", whereby the train crew had to be changed at the entrance to and exit from the classification yard. Road runs were no longer based on a day's work being considered as so many miles, but simply the hours it took to get from point A to point B. This change also had the effect of a huge reduction in clerical paperwork. We eliminated cabooses on all trains that had no backup movement nor special trains that carried nuclear materials for the US Department of Energy. Cabooses, it turns out, are not only very expensive to maintain, but can, under certain circumstances, become dangerous vehicles and hazardous to those occupying them.

CHAPTER IX

SPRINGFIELD TERMINAL

Prior to our efforts to expand to the West, Mr. Culliford had made an arrangement between the Springfield Terminal Railway, a short-line subsidiary of the Boston and Maine,[1] and the United Transportation Union (UTU) to operate the auto unloading facility at Ayer, Massachusetts. This facility was used primarily by Ford Motor Company as a central unloading point for all New England destinations. Cars were taken off auto-rack rail cars (15 per rail car) and reloaded onto the road transport vehicles for distribution.

The UTU had agreed to a rather unique contract in order to

---

1 The Springfield Terminal ran from Claremont, New Hampshire across the Connecticut River to Springfield, Vermont. The bridge across the river also carried vehicular traffic. The toll had been 25 cents for an automobile for many years. Dave Fink wanted to raise the toll to 50 cents, but New Hampshire's Governor Sununu had a fit and summoned Dave to his office in Concord.

"**What do you think of this**?" he blurted to Dave, pointing to engineering drawings laid out on his conference room table. "It's magnificent, but what exactly is it?" asked Dave. "**Well, it's a new bridge we are going to build right next to your bridge, and cars will have to pay no toll at all!**" Sununu continued triumphantly.

"I can't believe your generosity, Governor. When you build our new bridge, we will have King Charles to thank too! Because it was he who gave us exclusive rights to cross the Connecticut River both fifteen miles upstream and downstream from our present location!" The State of New Hampshire eventually purchased our old bridge for a tidy sum.

procure the exclusive employment rights to this work for their members. All work was to be performed on an hourly wage basis, and there were to be no onerous work rules attendant to the work. Although the unloading of the autos did not occur on the physical property of the Springfield Terminal Railway, an almost defunct branch line that ran from Charlestown, New Hampshire across the Connecticut River to Springfield, Vermont, nonetheless the railroads separate existence provided a legal shield for the protection of this labor contract.

We thought, what the heck, if the labor contract was valid, why would there be any reason that the Springfield Terminal's operations couldn't be expanded to other areas? So a portion of the Maine Central was leased to the Springfield Terminal, whereby the lessee gained the exclusive rights to the operation and maintenance of the leased property. The lease was approved by the ICC, as there could be no determination that the arrangement would reduce competition or be anything but advantageous to the customers on the leased portion of the MEC. The unions could not object because the work was still being performed under a validly negotiated contract.

That being successful, additional portions of the Maine Central Railway were leased, in several tranches, to the Springfield Terminal using the same logic. And then the process spread Westward to the Boston and Maine. Within a year both railroads were being operated completely by the Springfield Terminal, which hired the displaced employees of the Maine Central and B&M to augment the ranks necessary to perform the operations. These additional employees, of course, were now subject to the conditions of the UTU's Springfield Terminal labor agreement.

The employees of the Delaware and Hudson obviously saw the writing on the wall. When Guilford then proposed an additional expansion of the Springfield Terminal's operations to include the entire Delaware & Hudson property, the ICC pinball machine went "**TILT**"! The unions threw up ferocious objections of "Union Busting" in an election year (1988) and the politicians came out pandering in their favor. We suggested to Heather Gradison, Chairman of the ICC, that of our three railroads, the D&H was by far the financially weakest, and therefore most appropriate to receive this solution in order to preserve the viability of the underlying railroad.

To no avail. The ICC placed onerous conditions on the application that would not permit the D&H to become a profitable part of a unified Guilford Rail System. It took no more than an hour's consideration and deliberation to conclude that the Delaware & Hudson would soon become an albatross around our corporate neck, and that we would have to divest ourselves of it *tout de suite*. A short time later we filed bankruptcy proceedings in the Delaware Courts, where the D&H had been incorporated. After some time, the property was legally reorganized and sold to the Canadian Pacific Railway. Canadian Pacific thereupon invested over $150 million in the upgrading of the D&H, but to date, to my knowledge, has never been able to make a profit from its ownership. Just recently, Norfolk Southern (successor the N&W) announced that it would reacquire a significant portion of the D&H, another irony!

Relieved of the D&H, we now began the long process of recovering from the strike, catching up with the maintenance that had to be deferred due to dire financial straits, and refinancing our debt with a bank a little more sympathetic to our predicament than was Mellon Bank in Pittsburgh. There would be labor peace for a long time to come: as Dave put it to their representatives, "We didn't ask you to leave. And we didn't ask you to come back!" We could not be intimidated by threats, because we knew that we could operate the property with or without their co-operation.

Best of all, the size of the crew on a typical freight train was reduced from five to two. The savings accruing from these (and other changes) have been staggering. Since the end of our strike, we have had no year, even during the 2008 downturn, where the railroad has not been able to make a profit. And why is it so important for a railroad to make profit every year? Because most of the profit goes right back into the property in the form of investment in new equipment, improvement of track and signals, and increase of service to the customers who are thereby encouraged to ship more product over the railroad.

Lesson of Life: Labor relations have much in common with an overhead cam. Shaped like an upside-down "U", an overhead cam is a device that contemplates two very stable states, one on the left side at the bottom of the "U" and the other on the right side. To lift the cam up and over the top of the upside-down "U" takes tremendous effort to overcome the initial inertia as well as the steep grade. But once at the top, which represents the most unstable position in the scenario, it takes only a small bit of energy to push the cam, one way or the other, so that it falls down to one of the two stable positions.

In our situation, years, nay decades, of intimidation of weak managements by the various rail labor unions had produced a stasis equivalent to one of the stable cam positions. When financial necessity required us to take action to avoid the demise of our investment, we summoned the energy, imagination, and effort to move that cam to the other side of the "U". Once over the hump, a new stability emerged that will be very difficult, if not impossible, to reverse in the future.

We can take pride that our own efforts have endured to the benefit of the entire rail industry. You would be hard pressed to find a caboose anymore, anywhere in the country. Most trains now have two-man crews. Many anachronistic work rules (but not all) have been eliminated as well. Partially as a result of these changes, the railroad industry has been reborn and enjoys a new-found success and viability. As the little girl in the Shake'n Bake ad used to exclaim, "And we helped!"

CHAPTER X
RECONSTRUCTION

Once the arrangement with the Springfield Terminal had been put into place, the railroad was able to reinvest newly earned profits into upgrading the fleets of locomotives and rail cars, and overcoming deferred maintenance on the track structure. As a result of the strikes, three millstones had been removed: the work rules, of course; but also the non-producing Delaware & Hudson, as well as the contract with the State of Massachusetts to run the commuter train system on the North side of Boston. The "T" contract did nothing but put the Massachusetts State Government into a position to thwart our every effort to modernize the property. In effect, it left us in the position of subsidizing a losing proposition, year after year.

New projects were started that allowed the railroad to augment its traffic base. Increasing the height of the Hoosac Tunnel to nineteen feet meant that we could now import the tri-level auto-racks to Ayer for the Ford Motor Company. We improved the line between Ayer and Worcester so that a better connection could be made with CSX. Welded rail proliferated on our main lines, such that trains could move faster and more safely.

Of particular contention was the relationship with Amtrak, the government owned passenger rail company that had rights to run over our tracks between Springfield, Massachusetts and Montreal. As this line carried very little freight, we could not devote much of our resources, human or monetary, to improving this track. The speeds deteriorated to a point that the politicians decided that they had to invoke the principals of eminent domain. The Congress, in essence, expropriated a section of our track and gave it to our competitor, the Central Vermont Railway (at that time a subsidiary of the Canadian National). We retained the freight rights over the line, and were paid several million dollars compensation. We appealed this process all the way to the US Supreme Court but lost by a vote of six to three (Rehnquist, Scalia, and Thomas voting for us). The New England Central (successor to Central Vermont) has recently attempted to frustrate our efforts to provide competitive service by restricting our operations, but have been rebuffed by the Transportation Safety Board ("TSB", successor to the Interstate Commerce Commission).

And then there was Portland. For years, the people of Maine had been agitating for Amtrak to extend their service Northward from Boston, through New Hampshire, to Portland, Maine. In days of yore, there used to be two separate railroads running between the two cities, but once the Boston & Maine came into control of both of them, the less useful of the two lines was abandoned. It was way too late to salvage the abandoned line to create a dedicated passenger line. So Amtrak decided that, based upon their success in seizing our track for the *Montrealer*, they would force their way onto our freight-only right-of-way between Lowell and Portland (the track from Boston up to Lowell was owned by the MBTA, so we had no say as to its further use).

This section of rail line was one of the most important sections in our whole system, as it carried all the traffic destined to and from Maine and Eastern Canada. So we took the position that we would co-operate with Amtrak, but only on our terms: Any improvement in the tracks would be at their cost, and additional on-going maintenance that could be attributed to the need of keeping the track at 69 MPH would be at their cost, and improvements to the signaling, likewise. They wanted welded rail for the entire stretch, but wanted to take our old rail in trade. We said no, thanks, we'll keep the old rail, since we didn't ask you to come onto our line in the first place. We insisted, and prevailed, to be held harmless with respect to insurance, save for gross negligence on our part. We also insisted upon being in charge of the upgrades, the ongoing maintenance, and the dispatching of trains. The project went forward, was completed on schedule, and the operations have largely been smooth ever since. We are proud, as a host railroad, that Amtrak's on-time performance over our line between Boston and Portland is arguably the best in the country. Just last year, the Amtrak service has been extended to Brunswick, Maine.

More recently, we have gone into a joint venture with the Norfolk Southern. We created a 50–50 partnership, Pan Am Southern ("PAS"), to own and operate the Western portion of the Boston and Maine property. We contributed all the rail lines West of Ayer, and NS contributed sufficient funds to completely upgrade the line with welded rail, and in addition, to pay for a new auto-unloading facility at Ayer on the 100 acres we purchased from Sanvel, as well as a brand new inter-modal and auto-unloading facility in Mechanicsville, New York, on the land that used to be B&M's classification yard for the traffic interchanged with the D&H. Actual running of the trains on the PAS is contracted to the Springfield Terminal Railway. These improvements have produced higher traffic levels due to more reliable and more frequent service.

Another project on the PAS is the "Knowledge Corridor", between Springfield, Massachusetts and East Northfield, Massachusetts, near the Vermont border. PAS has entered into an arrangement for the State of Massachusetts to buy this track, have the Federal Government pay for its upgrade, so that the *Montrealer* could be restored to its original, faster, route. MBTA could, in the future, run commuter trains north from Springfield to service the various college towns. Again, PAS would retain all freight rights and be able to run trains at 40 MPH instead of ten.

Still another area of endeavor concerned the disposition of unused rail properties. As various lines have been abandoned, parcels of land previously used as rail yards in various cities have become available for sale or development. The most important of these has been Northpoint, an old B&M freight yard located in Cambridge just north of the Charles River. Consisting of approximately 43 acres, this piece of land was growing rapidly in value, but had no further use to the railroad, inasmuch as very little traffic any longer originated or terminated near downtown Boston. We knew it was growing in value because the property taxes kept going up!

We endeavored on several occasions to sell the entire yard to one party or another, but the economics in the last few decades of the 20th century were just not conducive. The history of Northpoint will be developed further, below, in Chapter XVI.

There are several other urban properties still ripe for development, not the least of which is the Maine Central yard adjacent to downtown Portland, Maine (recently sold), and a nice parcel in Portsmouth, New Hampshire. Our successful launching of the Northpoint project in Boston has provided us with the credibility to undertake these other ventures, as time and economics dictate. We have always relied on the wisdom reflected in the old adage, "If we build something of high quality, there is no question that it will sell well."

CHAPTER XI

"THIS IS TOMAHAWK N2387K": LEARNING TO FLY

Before I attempt to describe the Pan Am experience, I shall have to return many years to describe how I became involved in aviation. As a youngster, I was, from time to time, transported to school from Virginia in my father's DC-3. I got to know the pilots quite well, Walt Helmer and Art Ray. They allowed me to stand behind them in the cockpit and didn't mind me asking questions about the airplane or the procedures. In fact, over time they taught me quite a bit.

As a young adult, air transportation overtook rail transportation as the dominant mode in the early 1960s. For whatever reason, I became somewhat apprehensive of flying, though I recall no specific instance that invoked fear. Well, I take that back: one evening travelling on Allegheny Airlines from New Haven to Washington, its Convair made an intermediary stop in Philadelphia. As the plane started to taxi off the runway, all the electrical power failed, and we were told that there would likely be a delay before the trip could resume. This was quite disconcerting to me. I prevailed upon Sue that we should deplane and finish our trip to DC by train. Which we did.

Some years later, while I was involved in those various business start-ups, Sue meanwhile had become very proficient in several crafts, jewelry and textile weaving, and also excelled at the piano. Gradually, she tired of these various activities and also tired of my deeper involvement in business. What came to the fore was her desire to learn how to fly. She set out to find an instructor and, after several lessons in his Cessna 150 2-seater, she was so enthused that she went out and purchased her own Cessna 172RG. After some months, I suggested a trip to Florida to look at an old B-25 that was for sale. I had long been interested in this vintage of aircraft. So we set out, Sue, Harry Beech (her instructor) and I, and flew to Florida, Sue being the pilot and I being the rear seat passenger. On the return trip, approaching our intermediate destination in Wilmington, North Carolina, the weather deteriorated to the point that we were "scud-running", or making our way between a very low overcast and the ground. My impression, as a non-pilot, was that this was not very smart or safe, but Mr. Beech prevailed, and we pressed on towards Wilmington.

Mr. Beech was also not interested in using the transponder while flying in visual meteorological conditions (VMC, fair weather). This device sent out a signal that could be displayed on the monitor of the appropriate air traffic control center, such that other planes could be warned of the location and altitude of the "target". Really, just a safety freebie, even if one's own plane were not communicating with ATC. My wonder quickly morphed into concern that my wife was not receiving the best of instruction. What sealed my misapprehension was the flight that Mr. Beech took me on to allow me to see what was involved with flying. The first time out went without incident. On the second flight, however, he proceeded to show me how his little airplane could handle a "spin". This advanced maneuver basically involves stalling the aircraft so that it starts downwards with no forward airspeed or lift. It drops like one of those pods from a Chinese Elm. A very dizzying experience, to say the least, and quite terrifying to a novice. I later surmised that this exercise was designed to discourage me from wanting to learn to fly.

But these things had exactly the opposite effect. A month or so later, I stopped in at the New Haven Airport and arranged to take a flying lesson. I needed to confirm to myself that my wife was not being taught the best of procedures. I started out in a Piper Cherokee, also a simple single engine airplane. Tom Glista was my instructor; he worked for New Haven Airways, a small commuter operation. I enjoyed the instruction, easily passed the FAA written test for Private Pilot, and resolved to purchase my own airplane to finish off my training. I found a nice little 2-seat Piper Tomahawk and used New Haven Airways as my agent to purchase it. Within two months of starting, I had passed the FAA Practical test and earned the Private Certificate. This allowed me to fly anywhere, with passengers, in all but Instrument conditions. And I had satisfied my curiosity about Mr. Beech's unwarranted and sub-safe aeronautical practices. My opinions to that effect did not sit well with my wife.

Figure 8: Tomahawk N2387K.

My elation knew no bounds: the very next evening after getting my license, I flew my little Tomahawk up to Boston to attend a meeting involving our railroad business. I landed at Logan Airport after dark, a brand new challenge. I quickly learned to maintain my distance from the large commercial jets, any one of which could have blown me straight into Boston Harbor. The new freedom gained by flying one's own aircraft proved especially useful in our efforts to enter the rail industry. We could fly back and forth to Washington, or Pittsburgh, or Boston on a moment's notice; and the cost was really no more per mile than, say, renting a mid-sized car.

I also discovered that I had totally lost my fear of flying, and I figured out why: when one is simply a passenger in an airplane, one's frame of reference is always the ground. You sit in your seat, and when the plane takes off, you see the ground receding underneath you. At last you land and are re-united with *terra firma*. As pilot of an airplane, however, your frame of reference is no longer the ground, but the airplane itself: the pilot sits in his seat and, by applying the various controls, manipulates what he sees outside the windshield, somewhat like a video game, I suppose. Nothing disturbs the calm unity of the pilot and his seat in the cockpit, save for extreme turbulence, which is rare. Beryl Markham provides much the same insight in her classic *West with the Night.*[1]

Next on the aeronautical agenda was procuring an instrument rating, the ability to fly through the clouds under Air Traffic Control, and land safely at airports suffering poor weather conditions. The Tomahawk proved entirely adequate for this upgrade, as I had equipped it with the appropriate navigational instruments requisite to the task. Tom Glista led me through this additional training, and before long I was able to pass the practical test and be on my way through the bad weather, as necessary. This new ability expanded the usefulness of the airplane

1 Beryl Markham, *West with the Night* (Macmillan, 1942).

because the weather would no longer be an impediment, save for winter icing conditions.

A situation I fondly recall is the occasion when I was landing the Tomahawk at Washington's National (since renamed "Reagan") Airport. I was assigned Runway 33, and instructed to hold short of Runway 36, the main North-South Runway. To my surprise, the plane landing on Runway 36 was a Gulfstream II, N1929Y. My father's plane.

Now, the Tomahawk was a valiant little bird, but it did have drawbacks: maximum speed only 110 miles per hour; only one Passenger seat; a range of less than 500 miles; and, most inconvenient, the inability to handle icing conditions in the winter (especially a problem in the New England environment). So I "bit the bullet" and went searching for a more robust vehicle that would especially suit our growing business needs. The larger aircraft that most closely fit the bill was a Piper Aerostar. My next plane was purchased from Vee Neal, a distributer in Latrobe, Pennsylvania, not far from my great-grandfather Thomas' farmstead.

CHAPTER XII

"THIS IS AEROSTAR N602PC": MASERATI

The Piper Aerostar was originally the creation of Ted Smith, designer of the A-20, and the Aero Commander. It is a six-seat airplane with two turbo-charged reciprocating piston engines. Designed for speed, the Aerostar can cruise at over 250 knots and fly, pressurized, at an altitude of 25,000 feet. With an auxiliary fuel tank, it can achieve a range of over 1300 nautical miles. In addition, later variants were certified to fly through known icing conditions. These characteristics best satisfied the criteria I had sought: basically, a useful airplane that handled as well in the air as would a Maserati on the ground.

I needed additional training to fly the Aerostar: multi-engine operations necessitate familiarity with how to compensate for the failure of one engine, especially in the event of failure at take-off. Further, operations above 14,000 feet require familiarity with procedures necessary to overcome the failure of the pressurization system, and the resulting lack of oxygen. The Aerostar also had a more complicated fuel system than most planes. But, no matter, I passed the test and went about racking up over 3,600 hours in this great little aircraft.

As mentioned previously, the Aerostar became an invaluable tool during our labor challenges. I remember one day flying three round-trips

Figure 9: Aerostar N602PC .

between Pittsburgh, Pennsylvania and Binghamton, New York bringing fourteen volunteers (and their luggage) to work on the Delaware & Hudson.

As we pursued the purchase of parts of Conrail, we made heavy use of the Aerostar while canvassing the Middle West for corporate, media, and political support. One day we landed in Indianapolis. I deplaned and greeted the representative from the FBO. Dave Fink deplaned next. Pointing at the pilot (me) he yelled (in jest), "**Haven't I told you that when I step out of this plane, I want a red carpet at the bottom of the steps?!**" As we advanced towards the FBO, the lineboy queried, "Say, how did you get into corporate aviation?" I responded, "First I bought an airplane, then I bought a company." The lineboy was nonplussed.

This airplane made it possible to fly to anyplace in the country from the East Coast in one day, and only two legs. Alpine, Texas, for instance, where I had purchased a ranch, would for all intents and purposes have been unreachable without this vehicle. It was fast, efficient, and reasonably comfortable. Its negatives mostly consisted of the maintenance challenges that were posed by the very compact packaging of the engine components within the nacelles. One particular weakness was the unpredictable detachment of the output hose from the turbo-charger, which would automatically rob the engine of a considerable percentage of its power, with no way of compensating until a repair could be made on the ground. This failure was a little scary the first time, as neither the sudden change in noise nor the slight lurch were expected.

The only time that I have been really terrified in my own airplane was the occasion when I was flying to the West Coast with Louise, my second wife, and Jack Merry, the president of Vertical Systems. We had planned to stop in Spokane to have just such a turbo hose problem rectified. After taking off from Great Falls, Montana, our refueling point, we climbed normally aspirated to 14,000 feet, the highest we could attain with that defect. Unbeknownst and unforecast, we encountered severe icing while flying through the Cascade Mountains. The wings loaded up with rime ice and the aircraft's performance rapidly deteriorated. We sank below the Minimum Enroute Altitude as specified for that route on our chart. Luckily, we were in radar contact and able to ask for vectors to the nearest safe lower altitude where, hopefully, the ice would melt and be shed from the airfoil. At one point, I was convinced that I actually saw the terrain to one side. Eventually we landed in Kalispell, Idaho, where I needed a few hours to regain my composure.

It was an Aerostar that had set a speed record for flying around the world. I thought it would be possible to actually better that record (100+ hours) by at least 10 percent. My Aerostar, after all, had a greater range, thus requiring fewer fuel stops, and better speed performance. I convinced Tom Glista, my original instructor, to participate in the adventure. Months of planning, including co-ordination with the National Aeronautics Association and the Federation Aeronautique International

(FAI), to achieve the shortest permissible route (equal in distance to the length of the Tropic of Cancer/Capricorn), preceded our departure. I added and tested additional long-range navigation (Omega/VLF) and communication (HF) radio equipment.

We launched from Bangor, Maine, at exactly noon on the 30th of April, 1987. The first leg took us, just as planned, across the Atlantic Ocean to Manchester, England for our first refueling stop. There less than an hour, we were again airborne for Luxor in Egypt. The second leg took a bit longer than expected due to less strong tailwinds, but we landed still a tad ahead of the master plan. But after departing Luxor, our luck ran out. Tom was Captain on that leg; climbing through 17,000 feet on the way East over the Red Sea, the right engine suddenly lost oil pressure and much of its power output. Another blasted turbo hose. . . . Tom skillfully turned back towards Luxor, feathered the right engine, and landed safely. Upon further investigation, we determined that the turbocharger had actually disintegrated internally, a victim of the very fine sand particles that enshrouded much of the Middle East at that time of the year.

Our record attempt was a bust. Tom had to skedaddle back to his day job with the FAA in Washington. I was left with a huge challenge: abandon the aircraft then and there, or try to patch it up and return? I set out to find a tool kit in Luxor, no easy task. I also had to procure one of those four-inch hose clamps, which I finally found in a bicycle shop. With a little help from a friendly Egypt Air mechanic, I was able to take the turbo offline and return the engine to a reliable normally-aspirated condition. I hoped that the oil filter would protect the engine from any small metal particles that might have escaped the turbo after the disintegration.

So I went up to the control tower to ask permission to go on a little test flight, say, ten miles out and back, just to make sure everything was copacetic. No problem. "BUT! We'd like you to take off and land on the taxiway rather than on the runway!" An unusual request, to say the least. Why? "Because there is a performance of *Aida* in Luxor this weekend. If *you* crash, we will have to close the airport and none of the Sheiks who have been invited will be able to land in their Gulfstreams!" I complied with their conditions, without incident.

Next day, I started home. First leg was to Athens. Second leg to Gatwick Airport, South of London. Thence to Fair Oaks, where a new turbo was installed and the Aerostar returned to its normal condition. A short hop to Shannon, then across the Atlantic, non-stop to Bangor, where the adventure had started. But my problems paled in comparison to those endured by Louise: the day after our original departure, a huge ice storm attacked New England. Louise, alone with the dogs and horses, suffered four days without power in frigid late-winter conditions.

The experience left me with the Life Lesson: Don't attempt to fly through sand (or volcanic ash, for that matter). And it also convinced me that I had reached the envelope of the capabilities of the Aerostar. A piston powered airplane was just not as reliable, or fast, or comfortable as a turbine powered one. So, on to the next step.

CHAPTER XIII

"THIS IS CITATION N7TK": JET SET

If I were going to fly a jet powered aircraft, it would have to be certified for single-pilot operation. In 1989, this meant either a Cessna Citation I or Citation II (I did not feel that turbo-props, as opposed to pure jets, would be as useful, even though several were also certified single-pilot). I settled on a Citation I, as I rarely needed to carry more than five other people. One already equipped with Omega navigation was available in Oregon. The dealer from South Carolina and I met in Roseburg to fly the aircraft back to Orlando, Florida, for a pre-purchase inspection by Cessna. Several anomalies were discovered there, but subject to their correction and installation of my second Omega and HF from the Aerostar, I agreed to the acquisition.

My first flight as pilot-in-command of N7QJ was from the dealer's airport in Columbia, South Carolina, to Fort Rucker in Alabama, where I joined a group of helicopter enthusiasts for training to be judges in the International Precision Helicopter Competition to be held later in the summer in France. The Citation I (technically designated a C501) is a joy to fly: it is more docile and easier to handle than a Cessna single-engine 172. It practically lands itself. And although not very fast for a jet, this plane could fly as high as 41,000 feet, usually way above any inclement weather and/or turbulence. I was already planning to use the helicopter contest as a pretext for flying to Europe. My two Atlantic crossings in the Aerostar had built up my confidence in the ability to plan and successfully execute flights in the foreign environment.

The range of my new toy, however, was only about 1,300 nautical miles. So I was not able to fly directly to Europe, but rather had to assume a more circuitous route through Canada, Greenland, and Iceland. My first European jaunt was a great success, but left me searching for a way to augment the plane's range. Upon return, I contracted to have an auxiliary fuel tank installed in place of the potty, adding another 350 miles to the range. Subsequent flights across the Atlantic were then possible from Gander directly to Shannon, in Ireland. Several years later, another kit became available whereby another range extension was made possible by adding fuel capacity to a fattened wing, and by replacing the original Pratt & Whitney engines with those used on the Citation II. The added power also permitted an increase in the service ceiling to 43,000 feet, thus providing even more efficient fuel

Figure 10: Citation N7TK.

consumption. After these modifications were finished, I flew the plane to Wichita for repainting. I also used the opportunity to change the identification from N7QJ ("Quebec Juliet" being too much of a mouthful, and often misunderstood by ATC) to N7TK ("Tango Kilo", which just rolled off the tongue).

Happy now with this improved Citation, I was able to sell the Aerostar. The purchaser, however, was apparently unqualified to handle this aircraft: according to the accident report from the NTSB, he failed to properly reposition the flaps whilst executing a missed approach from an instrument landing at the Danbury, Connecticut airport. He also had not completed his Instrument Certification. He was injured in the mishap, and his wife was killed; the plane was totaled.

As of this writing, I have owned the Citation for 25 years, logged more than 4,800 hours, crossed the Atlantic Ocean more than 100 times and the Pacific twice, all safely and without mishap. Twice I have had the opportunity to fly non-stop from the West Coast to the East Coast, each time having more than 1.5 hours of fuel remaining in reserve upon landing. Of all the luxuries available in the world, this privilege I consider to be the most valuable: to be able to travel wherever, on a moment's notice if necessary, in speed and relative comfort, without the hassle of airport security, and then to be able to return just as soon as your business is complete. All this brings back the real joys of travel that have seemingly disappeared.

Yet it is not free, of course. I estimate the average cost to be about the same as First Class airline travel: there is the fuel, the insurance, the maintenance and the cost of recurrent training. Every year I must spend a week in Dallas at the CAE simulator in order to keep current and retain the right to fly this specific aircraft. By choosing single pilot, and I being the single pilot, I avoid the cost of hiring one (or more) crew, saving their weight in the performance calculations, not to mention the costs of food and lodging when on the road. The co-pilot's seat also makes a very handy place to set my flight computer, charts, checklist, snacks, and so forth. I am also not required to carry a cockpit voice recorder, since there is no-one really to talk to, nor the flight data recorder ("black box") because the total count of people on board is limited to six. Even less weight means even more fuel. Lesson of Flight: there is no such thing as too much fuel.

In 1996, my wife Pat and I took a fantastic vacation, spending 50 days flying around the world. The itinerary is included as Appendix "A". The highlight stops were Carthage, in Tunisia, Damascus, Madras (where Pat had resided for several years in the 1960s), Hanoi, Rikitea (in the most Eastern part of French Polynesia), and Easter Island. 29,051 nautical miles, 55 hours of flight later (with less than one hour in Instrument Meteorological Conditions), and anxious to see our dogs again, we arrived back to Westerly, our starting point. Charles, Amy and their son Cody met us in Phuket, Thailand but refused to stay at our fancy Amanpuri resort. We did entice them to a lovely meal brought

Figure 11: Totegegie Airstrip, Gambier Islands.

to the *sala* outside our room. Charles then accompanied us onwards to Hanoi, Halang Bay, and on to Macao where we visited them in neighboring Hong Kong.

Then in 1998, Pat and I had the opportunity to visit the Buddhist caves in Dunhuang, China. Our route from Helsinki took us to Aktubinsk in Kazakhstan,[1] then to Ürümqi in Western China, where we picked up a Chinese "navigator". He was there simply to make sure we didn't fly too close to Lop Nor, the rocket launching facility. Sarah Fraser accompanied us from Helsinki; she was preparing the photographic study and documentation of the cave interiors, a project sponsored by the Andrew W. Mellon Foundation. Apparently I am the first American ever to have landed at the Dunhuang Airport. We paid our landing, parking, and security fees, but I balked when they demanded a navigation fee. "You used our VOR on the airfield to find us here!" they insisted. "No," I shot back, "I used only GPS, an American navigation system which, by the way, is free for everyone in the world to use!" In typical Chinese fashion, we split the difference. On to Lanjou with the Bowens (AWM President) for lunch with the Vice Governor, Mr. Li. We retraced our route back to Helsinki, skipping only Dunhuang.

In 2004 Pat and I ventured Southward through Panama and Chile to visit the Falkland Islands, primarily as a gesture to honor British Prime Minister Margaret Thatcher for her stalwart protection of British sovereignty. Stanley, the capital, is a very windy place. We toured the nearby countryside by car and came upon what appeared to be the wreck of a military helicopter. Luckily, it was not at a place marked on our map as a potential mine field left over from the War (one is advised to carry such a map at all times). I retrieved a small piece that I think must be

1 I visited the Weather Office to obtain a briefing for the next leg of our journey. The chart showing Winds Aloft, I was surprised to find, had been hand-drawn and colored!

part of a fuel injection valve. Our return route provided the opportunity for a week's stay in Punta del Este, Uruguay, a lovely vacation town on the South Atlantic. Thence on to the Dominican Republic for a meeting with the Pan Am Board of Directors.

Absolutely the best trips of all have been those with Pat's children and grandchildren. Carla and her family have accompanied us to Italy, to the primeval forests at Bielowicz in Poland, to France, to the famous English gardens, and to Denmark. Charles convinced us to take his family to the beautiful Island of Muhu in Estonia. Nat has spent several vacations skiing with us in Switzerland. These journeys usually end up returning through Iceland, where traditionally we have landed in Reykjavik and spent the night at the Holt Hotel, consuming quantities of delicious gravlax (marinated salmon) and copious amounts of Aquavit (a Scandinavian schnapps). Not to forget the most educational trip with Jay and James to Russia to visit World War II battle sights at Voronezh, Kursk, and Stalingrad.[2] On the way back we also stopped at Munich, to visit the horrifying death camp at Dachau, and Berlin, with a side trip to the rocket launching facility at Pennemunde. We landed at Templehof Airport in Berlin, the destination of the famous Cold War airlift. Unfortunately, its use as an airport has since been discontinued. As my own education was so enhanced by travel, it has given me great pleasure, pride and satisfaction to be able to provide the same benefits to the next generations.

On the more practical side, the Citation had replaced the Aerostar as the principal mode of corporate transportation for the railroads. Although used nowhere near as heavily as was the Aerostar during the strikes, the Citation proved to be efficient and reliable as a means of

2 In Stalingrad we stayed at the Hotel Volgograd. Jay, James and I each had a single room. Each room had its own private telephone number. Promptly at 10 p.m. each evening, ring, ring, ring… "Hello?"—"You like nice Russian girl?" We will never know James' response.

saving executive time and the additional costs of accommodations in the case where round trips in one day were possible. Occasionally we were also in a position to offer a ride (properly compensated) to a politician, for example, the time we returned John McCain to Washington from Manchester, New Hampshire after a dinner speech. Dave was able to bend his ear for almost two hours. Citation usage finally picked up somewhat when we became interested in purchasing Pan Am out of bankruptcy.

CHAPTER XIV

PAN AM

One day it came to my attention, and I don't honestly remember how (perhaps I had heard it on the radio, the same way I heard Mr. Fishwick talk about the D&H), that the second iteration of Pan Am was in bankruptcy and was attempting to develop a re-organization to try a third time. You might remember that the original Pan American Airways, founded by Juan Trippe, could no longer make ends meet in the late 80s due to their inability to compete within the United States because of their unfortunate merger with National Airlines. National had been saddled with onerous labor contracts for quite some time. The straw that had "broken the camel's back" was the disastrous sabotage of Pan Am's Flight 103 over Lockerbie, Scotland in December, 1988. Libyans were later called to account for planting the bomb that took down the aircraft.

After Pan Am went into bankruptcy, a group of airline-savvy entrepreneurs resurrected Pan Am as a low-cost start-up catering primarily to the tourist trade between New York, Florida, and California. They purchased a fleet of the new Airbus, manufactured by the Europeans and allegedly more efficient than the Boeing aircraft favored by the original Pan Am. They hoped to augment their operations by merging with Carnival Airlines, the air subsidiary of the cruise ship company. But, for whatever reason, the second Pan Am floundered and after only a few years sank back into bankruptcy. The Airbus fleet was repossessed, and the hapless skeleton was left with two older Boeing 727s and one (engineless) Boeing 737. They operated out of a hangar at the North end of the Fort Lauderdale, Florida International Airport, and were reduced to flying occasional charters for travel companies and for the US Department of Justice (prisoner transfers).

Mr. David Banmiller, the surviving president, sent me whatever useful information I requested about the company, and after some careful planning about how an airline could be incorporated into a transportation company that heretofore dealt primarily with railroads, we made the decision to purchase the bankrupt entity and give it a third life. By now, we had achieved a high degree of expertise in the application of the Railway Labor Act, which covered not only railroads, but also airlines. The reason for this duality sprang from the origins of airlines themselves: TWA, for instance, started as a subsidiary of the Pennsylvania Railroad, a combination that allowed for the innovative cross-country service whereby one could fly in the daytime and connect with a night train to shorten the entire trip to two days instead of three or four. Likewise, Boston Maine Airways started as a joint venture between the Boston and Maine Railroad and the Maine Central Railway, and established routes from Boston up into Maine and Nova Scotia. Amelia Earhart was involved in this start-up and had the rank of Vice President at the B&M. Boston Maine Airways became Northeast Airlines, with routes between New England, Washington, and Florida (remember the "Yellowbirds"?) Northeast Airlines was eventually absorbed into Delta.

Other synergies that we thought we could bring to bear involved sharing mechanical resources, such as small cranes that could be used to remove and re-install aircraft engines, and fuel trucks. And any plane that had to be defueled for maintenance reasons would not in our case create a useless hazardous waste: the fuel could readily be re-used in one of our locomotives. The strikes had taught us extreme frugality, so that these innovations came easily to us. The ability to aggregate our jet fuel purchases with our diesel purchases for the locomotives would also give us the purchasing power to minimize our costs. Finally, the executive overhead could be minimized by creating dual responsibilities on each side of the transportation scale.

So off we flew to Fort Lauderdale to assess the property. Seeing no Herculean obstacles, we formulated our bid to purchase the assets of the Debtor. In charge of the sale was the Chief Judge of the United States Bankruptcy Court for the Southern District of Florida, Judge Jay Cristol. Judge Cristol was no ordinary judge. He was intimately familiar with aviation, having flown for the Navy in World War II (his actual aircraft hangs in the Museum at the Pensacola Naval Air Station). He had further experience as Captain, flying the Boeing 727 for Eastern Airlines.

The day of his hearing arrived. The courtroom was packed with people interested in the future of Pan Am. Judge Cristol introduced the hearing, then summoned Dave Fink and me to approach the bench. In hushed tones that the audience could not hear, the Judge presented to each of us one of those little Pan Am overnight kits that passengers used to receive, with the slippers and blinders. He made a little speech about how great it was that the Pan Am name was going to survive and how he was so honored to be part of the process. As the two of us returned to our seats in the front row, we knew that the approval was already a "done deal".

Approval came rapidly, so we grabbed the reins and went about taming our new steed. First on the agenda was a "*thank you*": we renamed one of the two 727s the *Clipper A. Jay Cristol* and invited the Judge and his family for a ride. A quick round trip to the Dade-Collier Training and Transition airstrip west of Miami. The Judge was offered the left seat and proceeded to make a near-perfect landing, to cheers from those of us riding as passengers. When the FAA heard of this antic, they were not particularly pleased. . . .

Figure 12: *Clipper A. Jay Cristol.*

We learned quickly that it was not going to be so easy to run this airline simultaneously with running the railroads when such a distance separated the two activities. In order to gain effective control we resolved to relocate the airline closer to home. We rented a large hangar at the Pease International Airport in Portsmouth, New Hampshire, surplus from the Air Force when Pease had been a B-52 base. Our marketing strategy, in any case, was to service "satellite" airports near large cities rather that compete head-to-head with the larger airlines in the traditional near-city-center airfields. Pease was an ideal surrogate for Boston. Our first scheduled route, then, provided daily service between Pease and Sanford, Florida (Walt Disney and Cape Kennedy being the primary tourist attractions). Later, service was extended to Gary, Indiana (outside Chicago), East St. Louis, and to Pittsburgh. We handled this system with a fleet of seven Boeing 727s. These planes were older and less efficient with respect to fuel consumption, but the purchase price for each was correspondingly more favorable.

Clipper Service on our Pan Am was all coach, but we did make the seats more comfortable by increasing the "pitch" (distance between seat rows) by about four inches. We forewent meal service in favor of drinks and snacks. This allowed us to do away with the rolling food carts, which present a real hazard to passengers and crew alike in turbulence. Friendly flight crew personnel were also an obligatory component of our strategy.

As things settled down, I took it upon myself to undergo the training necessary to fly the Boeing 727 as Captain. The training took place between several ragtag simulator facilities in Miami. As I was the first person on the roster, even before the bankruptcy was finalized, I declared myself Number One in Seniority, thus avoiding any childish labor disputes about when and where I could fly. The hardest part of training was the ground school, which taught the various aircraft systems such as hydraulic, electrical, fuel and so forth. The simulator, although cranky and unpredictable at times, was easier to master. Clay Faulkner was my instructor; he had been a check pilot on the previous Pan Am. When I graduated to the real airplane, Clay was the one who acted as my co-pilot for the training flights. Although I passed the FAA flight test without too much trouble, I did not yet feel totally comfortable landing the actual aircraft. Eventually, one of the Flight Engineers gave me an important hint: cut the power on the middle engine while 100 feet high in the landing zone. This worked perfectly, and Clay's method, using too much power, was abandoned.

In the next several years, I flew regularly scheduled flights, for example, Pease to Sanford and back, as well as charters from Boston to the Caribbean (Jamaica and Aruba) and to Mexico. I accumulated about 180 hours in the 727. I enjoyed the work, although it was quite a bit more dogmatic than flying one's own aircraft. The main difference was the necessity to work with two other crewmembers; to communicate clearly with one another, and to follow the FAA approved procedures as closely as possible. "CRM", or Cockpit Resource Management, has become a big theme in the FAA's campaign to improve aircrew performance and maximize safety. If one sees someone doing something improperly, the idea is to challenge them to the point they must respond, acknowledge, and then correct whatever was performed improperly. In earlier years, the captain's seniority would often intimidate those of lesser rank into keeping quiet, which sometimes led to disastrous consequences. By contrast, flying alone as a single pilot, the trick is to keep challenging one's self that everything is going according to proper method.

Meanwhile, my wife Pat decided that she wanted to train to be a flight attendant. We tucked into the Marriott Residence near Pease, with our dogs, one cold winter, and she attended the daily classes in Tower D of our hangar. Ready for her check ride, she was scheduled to fly on a round-trip from Pease to Sanford and back, then on to Bangor. I was the captain that day (by design). She will tell you that it is not easy work, walking back and forth, balancing a tray of drinks, answering questions, and generally keeping up a cheery disposition. By the time we returned to Pease she was thoroughly exhausted, so was excused from flying the last leg. Pat's check ride flight was her last. But what a great experience!

Our fleet expanded when we found that United Airlines mothballed a whole slew of 727s in the California desert. We purchased ten of these, hoping to create a fleet large enough to re-enter the international market in the Caribbean and South and Central America. We also purchased two flight simulators from United's training center in Denver. These we set up in our own facility in Sanford, Florida, where we not only were able to keep our own flight crews current, but also able to sell time to other airlines. Eventually, we resold these simulators to FedEx.

One advantage to owning an airline is that you can charter your own plane, at cost, if the need arises. Knowing this, my wife and I planned an excursion to Reykjavik, Iceland at the end of December in the year 2000, to celebrate the Millennium. We believed that it should be celebrated at the end of the 2000th year, not at the end of the 1999th year, as did most. So with Captain Russ Jester at the helm, we departed Pease with 90 or so friends and arrived in Reykjavik some hours later in time for a beautiful buffet at our favorite Holt Hotel. The highlight of the flight was the disclosure by Nat to his mother that his wife Zeena was pregnant. I immediately snatched the plane's intercom to make the important announcement: "We have discovered that there is a stowaway on our plane!" New Year's Eve ended with one of the most spectacular fireworks display one could imagine. The entire sky over Reykjavik was ablaze for over an hour. We watched from our balconies as the 21st century arrived with a bang. Next day, Captain Jester and crew, wearing their Nordic horned hats, flew us back to Pease. We called this junket "The Mellonium". And so proclaimed a t-shirt designed and distributed by Amy, emblazoned with the Icelandic Puffin, in a choice of sizes and colors.

CHAPTER XV

BOSTON MAINE AIRWAYS

A year or so into our ownership of Pan Am, we thought we needed a method to transport equipment by air, such as a jet engine. We pursued the purchase of a CASA, a small freighter made by the Spanish. A company in California, Arlington Leasing, had two such aircraft, and as it turned out, the company was itself for sale. It had its own Part 135 Certificate, which we thought could be used to our advantage. We purchased the company and renamed it Boston Maine Airways, after the original airline that had been set up under the aegis of our two railroads in the 1930s.

Unlike Pan Am, this company came with no flight crews. We therefore had the opportunity to develop a commuter operation by adding the BAE Jetstream to the certificate and flying the Jetstream with non-union flight crews, which we would hire, and train. The Jetstream was an older turbo-prop airplane with nineteen seats (therefore requiring no flight attendant). It was being phased out by other airlines in favor of newer pure-jet powered "Regional" airliners, such as that manufactured by Embraer in Brazil. We made a deal to buy ten of the Jetstreams that were sitting idle at the Kingman, Arizona airport. One by one they were ferried back to the East Coast, upgraded as necessary, repainted in the Pan Am livery, and given a Clipper name. We named the Jetstreams after rivers, for example the *Clipper Shenandoah*.

The "Pan Am Connection" commenced operations when enough of the ten were ready for service that would provide sufficient redundancy taking into account normal maintenance rotations. We picked routes of opportunity, the most successful being from Hanscom Field in Bedford, Massachusetts, just outside of Boston, to Trenton, New Jersey. For several years we also flew subsidized routes from Baltimore to Hagerstown and Cumberland, in Maryland.

Then along came "9/11". This one event, which arguably has transformed our entire nation, certainly had immediate and debilitating effects on the airline industry as a whole, and on small operations like Pan Am in particular. For a while, people became more reluctant to travel by air. Then, as our nation prepared for military operations in the Middle East, the price of fuel increased dramatically. Insurance premiums skyrocketed due to the perceived threat of further terrorist incidents. On top of these factors, security procedures were implemented at airports that caused difficulties for scheduling departures and further inconveniences to passengers.

It became apparent to us that Pan Am, with its gas-guzzling 727 fleet, would be hard-pressed to turn a profit under these new financial constraints. Further belt tightening was in order. If we could attain certification for the 727 under the Boston Maine Airway certificate, then these planes too could be operated by crews not associated with the various unions. This major saving could mitigate the effects of the "new reality."

To accomplish this goal, Boston Maine Airways would have to upgrade its certificate to Part 121, similar to Pan Am's. These changes would entail months and months of effort, as operational and maintenance procedures had to be updated to a higher standard. Eventually we succeeded and were allowed to put one 727 onto the newly upgraded certificate. We then applied to transfer three more from the Pan Am certificate over to BMA. More time, more paperwork.

Then, the most unimaginable and devastating catastrophe befell our company. John Nadolny, Chief Counsel to all our companies and their affiliates, was found to have falsified documents provided as part of a settlement with some Pan Am employees. The company had failed to timely make an installment payment, which triggered the investigation. It was not as if the company did not have the funds to make this rather modest payment. But Mr. Nadolny took it upon himself, for reasons that are still totally obscure and not understood, to generate false surety bond showing that the company was in a better financial position than reality dictated. Mr. Nadolny was found guilty in a New Hampshire legal proceeding, and thereafter spent six months in prison.

The unions then seized on this tragedy to influence the Federal Aviation Administration to put the kibosh on BMA's application to move more aircraft from Pan Am to BMA. Unjust and unfounded accusations against Pan Am's executives were brought to bear and had the effect of burying our company in long-term legal battles that, until completed, would make it impossible to restore our revoked certificate. The company's finances could not outlast this morass, so we resolved to cease airline operations all together, sell (or scrap) our fleet of airplanes, abandon our maintenance hangar at Pease, and return to railroading as our chief line of endeavor.

But neither Pan Am nor Boston Maine Airways went bankrupt. Pan Am continued to whittle down its inventory of spare parts. A new business was started to capitalize on the famous brand name (second only to Coca Cola, apparently, in world-wide trademark recognition). A full line of related travel items, such as the iconic flight bag, have built upon a nostalgic appreciation of air travel in bygone days. These items are for sale over the Internet (see www.panam.com) and through recognized retail chains, such as Nordstrom's.

Boston Maine Airways reduced its fleet to one Jetstream. This aircraft was recently traded for another Jetstream that had younger engines and a corporate configuration. It is used for executive travel and can also be leased on charter. Additionally, several mechanical operations have been developed to capitalize on the experience of our mechanical employees. These include rehabilitating batteries, building train control devices that signal the brake pressure from the rear end of a freight train, building power units for locomotives that provide for warming the engine oil and keeping the batteries charged while the main engine of the locomotive is shut down to save fuel.

Some years ago, we also renamed our railroads from the "Guilford Rail System" to "Pan Am Railways". The original Pan Am logo, the globe with the wing, adorns each and every newly repainted locomotive. It has replaced the Guilford rolling "G", designed by Brenda Huffman of Essex, Connecticut, which symbol represented the unification of our three New England railroads. We are extremely proud of our name, proud of our company, and especially proud of all our employees who have worked so long and hard to make our company a success.

CHAPTER XVI

NORTHPOINT

Our three railroads were endowed with substantial amounts of surplus land resulting from the more efficient operational procedures developed over the years; from the duplication of facilities deriving from the combination of the three properties; and from the changes in types of traffic being hauled by the railroads. One of the largest pieces of excess land sat at the very Eastern tip of Cambridge, just across the Charles River from Downtown Boston. This land had been a large freight yard for the termination of various goods arriving at Boston. One section had been devoted entirely to the operations of the Railway Express Agency, the precursor to UPS and FedEx.

Consisting of over 43 acres of flat land that had been created decades earlier by filling tidal lowlands, this yard had been sitting idle for several decades by the time we purchased the Boston and Maine Railroad in 1983. Small parcels had been leased on a short-term basis (30 day cancellation by the railroad) to various entities solely as a means of recouping the property taxes levied on the property by the City of Cambridge. The yard also spanned the town line to include several small slivers of land in Somerville, as well as about an acre of Boston proper.

The land, known as "Northpoint" to the City of Cambridge, had obvious developmental value. However, we had neither the time nor the excess capital to enter the field of land development for the first ten years of Guilford's existence. Several preliminary concepts were drawn up, including one by the Architect I. M. Pei, to demonstrate the capability of the land to hold over two million square feet of combined residential and commercial real estate.

In our innocence, we created a partnership with Messrs. Farmer and Flyer, Boston developers who had experience dealing with the MBTA (Metropolitan Bay Transportation Authority, the agency that ran the busses, subways, and commuter trains). The MBTA connection was important because the Northpoint land was adjacent to the Northern terminus of the Green Line, an older streetcar facility in Eastern Cambridge. But as a result of a lawsuit from the Conservation Law Foundation, the MBTA had just entered into a consent agreement to mitigate some perceived *faux pas*. They agreed to extend the Green Line to Medford. Such a new extension would force the line to go right by Northpoint and, more importantly, force the MBTA to build a brand new Lechmere Station on Northpoint land. In addition, the extension would have to pass over the Fitchburg commuter line on a bridge that was still owned by the B&M. Co-operation with the MBTA would have to be a crucial component to the success of developing Northpoint.

The partnership with Farmer and Flyer was not lasting. Their architect developed a mediocre scheme in terms of city block layout and transportation infrastructure. More importantly, our partners failed to meet several contractual deadlines. We pulled the plug. They pursued an unsuccessful lawsuit to recover what they perceived to be improvements to the property resulting from their specific efforts.

We then sought advice as to how to find a more reliable partner. After consulting with Governor Weld and his colleague Bob Cordy, we learned of a very reputable developer, a partnership by the name of Spaulding and Slye. Our meetings with the principals of this firm quickly convinced us of their expertise and integrity. We drew up the necessary partnership agreements and commenced anew. A talented architectural firm from Toronto, Greenberg Consultants, created a new master plan that featured a linear community park in the middle of the development. We knew this would sell well with the City of Cambridge.

David Vickery was one of the principals of Spaulding and Slye. In earlier years he had worked for the Planning Board in Cambridge and had garnered the trust of the city officials, including Bob Healy, the City Manager. With my own City Planning background, I was able to accompany David to meetings with several influential Planning Board members, and mollify their concerns that our company actually could produce a development of high quality that would fit into Cambridge's own visions of its future. In spite of some vocal (and predictable) opposition from several local community agitators, our plans were accepted by unanimous vote not only of the Planning Board, but also of the Cambridge City Council (the legislative body that created policy for the city).

The principals of Spaulding and Slye were easy to get along with and seemed to share our values with respect to the quality we sought in the end product. What they didn't share with us, however, was knowledge of their negotiations to be bought out by the Chicago development behemoth Jones, Lang, LaSalle ("JLL"). When the ink had dried, we were presented with a *faît accompli* in which our trusted friends were ruled by outsiders whose goals and methods soon brought us into perpetual conflict. No longer were the Spaulding and Slye folks calling the shots. They were taking their orders from JLL, and not really appearing to be happy about it.

To illustrate the new arrogance we encountered, consider JLL's decision to hire the well-known landscape architecture firm of Michael Van Valkenburgh Associates, Inc. from New York. I travelled to meet the principals, was shown their most recent effort near the World Trade Center, and immediately developed a suspicion that we might be dealing with some slicksters that would advance their own reputations at the expense of a highly refined and sensitive treatment of our Northpoint centerpiece. Nonetheless, they were hired. Their initial plan caused me considerable concern: it attempted to include too many features, too close together, and lacked the sense of peace and quiet that a city dweller might expect when visiting a park for respite. "Trust us!" pleaded Matthew Urbanski, one of the Principals. "I'll let you know when I do!" I shot back. Matt also suggested we purchase all the trees from a nursery owned by his relative in Jersey. "I don't think so, Matt. I've got all those same trees growing on my property in Lyme, Connecticut. And I've got all those boulders that you want to place as steps around the water feature. I'll deliver them to Northpoint myself." And subsequently I did deliver four boulders to the site from my farm in Connecticut, one per trip on my 16-foot trailer. Glacial souvenirs from the last Ice Age.

One day, Lisa Sarafin, by now an employee of JLL, brought a set of plans for the park to my home in Connecticut to seek approval for further refinement. In spite of my earlier admonitions, the basic clutter had not disappeared from the concept. There were hills, but the slopes were too steep. There were trees, but too many to allow for any vistas. The Eastern end of the park ended in sort of a point: a raised plinth with trees on three sides. My wife commented, "You've created a nice little rape zone…." We suggested a few more "modifications", which Lisa dutifully took back to her masters. In the end, the park turned out to be a beautiful focal area for the Northpoint development, thanks to our perseverance.

Northpoint was carved into 23 or so lots. We needed an anchor building to show the real estate world that the project was real. We settled on two residential buildings of condominiums to get the project rolling. The *pro-formas* spewed forth. JLL wanted to arrange the financing, for which they would, of course, charge a percentage in addition to a finder's fee. What, we queried, would happen if the buildings were built and no-one showed up to buy? Who would carry the financing charges? Being the 75 percent owner in the partnership, our company could not stand a long drought. It disappointed JLL to no end when I decided to finance the construction myself. There went all those fees that they had calculated into their return. Of course along came the 2008 financial crisis in the midst of our construction. Most of the advance commitments to purchase just vanished. The JLL program would have spelled disaster; our solution allowed us to weather the financial storm. In the end, I broke even on the investment.

We named the lots after the phonetic alphabet used in aviation: Alpha, Bravo, Charlie, and so forth. JLL recoiled in horror. Nonetheless, Sierra and Tango became the names of our two condominium buildings: Sierra consisted of 99 duplexes, while Tango contained 230 mixed duplexes and flats. The two face one another across Earhart Street, named for the aviatrix.[1] Construction lasted more than two and one half years, as expected, and went fairly smoothly save for the slight disaster in Tango involving a ruptured plumbing line high up in the tower end, water cascading down into lower floors and causing considerable damage. Luckily, our insurance covered the costs. CBT Architects from Boston designed Sierra; architectsAlliance (*sic.*) from Toronto designed Tango. Both buildings turned out beautifully, exceeding our highest expectations.

But the process of finishing these structures revealed a gigantic flaw in our relationship with our new partners, JLL. At every turn, in every budget proposal, every new initiative or effort was

Figure 13: Tango and Sierra at Northpoint.

1 Another street in Northpoint, Childs Street, will be named after the famous TV chef Julia Childs.

jaundiced by the application and expectation of fees. To the point that JLL's business model was predicated on milking the project of fees rather than completing the development and moving on to another project. We, their 75 percent partner, had, in effect, become the customer. So it came to a head in an acerbic meeting of the partners: we refused to rubber stamp the next year's budget without substantial revisions to our relationship. The matter ended up in court, and was finally resolved when we were able to find a more reasonable partner willing to buy out the JLL interest for the $30 million that they had invested in their (and by acquisition, Spaulding and Slye's) total efforts. Lesson of Life: Don't put up with Malarkey.

Tom O'Brien, along with the Canyon Group, from California, with the basketball star Magic Johnson as one of the major investors, stepped in to replace Jones Lang LaSalle. A new 300+ unit apartment structure on parcel N (we would have called it "November") is, as of this writing, nearing completion. Driven by results rather than fees, we have taken heart that the project will now flourish as it becomes more and more apparent that Northpoint has become a major focal point in the ultimate development of the City of Cambridge.

Pam Am sold its remaining interest in Northpoint to its partner Canyon Group in November, 2014.

CHAPTER XVII

THE LAND

I have always loved the land: the open countryside, the fields, the woods and forests, the rivers and streams, the open skies and distant mountains. I think this appreciation came from my father, by osmosis. He spent many summers in England, much of the time foxhunting (a sport that never had any appeal to me). When he started collecting English Art in the 1940s, most depicted rural scenes and the rural way of life. When these pictures hung in our house in Virginia, it became hard to differentiate between the contents of the pictures, and the actual countryside seen out through the windows.

Rokeby was the name of the farm in Virginia purchased by my father for his mother. She never lived there. When my father first married, he and Mary moved from Pittsburgh to Oak Spring, an adjacent property across the county road (Route 623) from Rokeby. They periodically added more tracts to this nucleus: Loughborough, Milan Mill, and so forth. Eventually the entire contiguous estate comprised in excess of four thousand acres. It was situated in the middle of foxhunting territory, and many of the fences were modified to accommodate jumping hunters in the chase. Goose Creek meandered through the property on its gentle course to the Potomac.

My father loved to walk, and sometimes he would invite me along. He showed me the fox dens, with two separate entrances. And the ground-hog holes that became hazards to the horses and cattle. As wonderful as were the sights, I also came to appreciate the smells: the decaying fallen trees in the woods, the daffodils in the spring, the skunks' warning blasts. Once there arose a rabies scare: carried by the red fox, a bite could be lethal if not treated immediately. My father would carry a rifle on his outings for protection.

After leaving home for boarding school and college, I lost touch with the countryside. Only in my twenties and free of the academic demands on my time did I again start to yearn for open space. We lived in Guilford, Connecticut, right on Long Island Sound at the time. The open waters created their own landscape, of course, but it could only be ventured upon in a boat. As mentioned earlier, our half-acre lot, even with a new contemporary house, did not totally satisfy the urge to be nearer the land.

Freddy Sigler, my brother-in-law, had a great idea. He was a house builder and developer in Northern New Jersey. He and his family visited us frequently in Guilford. Freddy suggested that we hire a small airplane and, armed with the appropriate US Geodetic Survey map, fly along the shore of Long Island Sound, then up the Connecticut River, to find a piece of land that might be suitable for a more rural lifestyle than the one we enjoyed. We did just that. The most promising "targets" were along the Connecticut River, which was far less developed than the Long Island Sound shoreline. We later learned that this was because the river had until the 1960s been highly polluted by urban and industrial runoff further upstream, primarily from the mills in Hartford, Springfield, and Northampton.

Four or five X's ended up on our survey. We rated them informally as to desirability, and then sought ownership information from records in the appropriate town halls. The most appealing property was in the Town of Lyme. It was owned by a John Bross and consisted of approximately 340 acres at the confluence of the Eight Mile River and the

Connecticut River. Mostly wooded, it included a few small fields, a small cove known as the "Abigail", and a magnificent precipice, 150 feet straight up, over the Connecticut River that was known as Joshua Rock. Joshua had been the chief of a local Indian tribe.

I wrote or phoned Mr. Bross (I can't remember which) to ask if he possibly had any interest in selling all, or part of, his holdings. It turned out that he did. His mother, Mrs. Casalis, still lived in one of the four houses on the property, but John himself had never lived there, being an employee of the US Government at a large facility near Langley, Virginia.[1] We resolved to meet some weeks later at the property in Lyme. John had determined that he would be willing to part with 271 acres, but wanted to retain the remainder, including his mother's house. Being that the acres offered were the most valuable of the whole piece, and that the Seller was under no obligation or compunction to sell, we quickly agreed to his asking price of $625,000. Issues of water rights from the property to be sold, as well as obligations for the upkeep of the common driveway, were quickly resolved. We summoned attorneys in Stamford to prepare all the necessary papers, the deal was signed, and the property became ours.

Yet, even though we now owned arguably one of the most beautiful pieces of land in all of Connecticut, Sue and I were not ready to undertake the challenge of designing yet another residence. The two existing houses that conveyed were both old, run-down and pretty much ill-suited to our contemporary tastes. So the land just sat there . . . and sat there . . . and sat there, year after year. Cyrus Murphy was permitted to lease the Brick House in exchange for keeping an eye on the property. From time to time we would take a picnic to Lyme, sit atop Joshua Rock, or under the majestic swamp maple adjacent to the old frame River House.

1 Coincidentally, John Bross had been a member of the Office of Strategic Services (OSS) in World War II, where he knew my father.

I developed the notion, nonetheless, that the entire piece of land should be protected from development. After much negotiation with the Department of Environmental Protection of the State of Connecticut ("DEP"), we came to agreement that the land would be preserved in perpetuity through a grant of a scenic easement to the DEP, retaining only the rights to use the existing residential structures, and to use the land for agricultural, forestry and recreational purposes. The agreements were signed at the end of December, 1968. Governor Ella Grasso literally signed the agreement on her deathbed, one of her very last official acts.

Here is some free legal tax advice, NOT!: A scenic easement in favor of the State of Connecticut, or a town, or an environmental group like the Nature Conservancy, represents a charitable donation recognized by the Internal Revenue Service as a valid deduction against one's taxable income. In effect, the US Government is subsidizing the gift by permitting this tax treatment. Those in higher income brackets receive proportionally more benefits because they avoid the income tax on the amount equivalent to the appraised value of the gift. In addition, capital gain taxes are avoided on any appreciated value realized since the purchase of the asset. Real dollars saved, in other words. This benefit provides strong incentive to save land, beyond just the feeling of doing something that is also very worthwhile.

The donation of the scenic easement on the land in Lyme, as well as others described below, have for the most part been made to a State or state-sponsored institution. I will not make such a contribution to groups like the Nature Conservancy or Sierra Club because I have little confidence that they, unlike say the State of Connecticut, will be around forever. Furthermore, some of these groups have made insider deals directly in violation of the terms of the original donation. When the state is the steward, it is unlikely to want to suffer the slings and arrows of popular condemnation for mistreating a property which they have been entrusted to safe-keep. Sometimes political pressure can be very useful.

The various entrepreneurial activities described in previous chapters more or less forced the Lyme property into the background of our consciousness. Sue's sister Sally had remarried in the early 70s and we were able to rent the River House to them as a summer residence. Sally's younger daughter Kirsten was married there in 1990. Sue and I divorced in 1982, so all plans for any residence there flew out the window. But I retained title to the Lyme land and felt satisfied that it had been properly preserved forever.

A new marriage brought new interests into focus. Louise, my second wife, was Wendy Whitney's younger sister. She had previously lived in Phoenix and was a keen equestrian. This was the time of my entry into the railroad business. My focus was further North, and so we decided to relocate from Guilford to New Hampshire. Louise found a small farm near the center of Amherst, half wooded and half set up for horses, including a beautiful barn and several paddocks. We lived there throughout the 1980s, but also were enticed by the possibility of someday returning to Connecticut to live and enjoy the beautiful property in Lyme. The land in Amherst was too small and already too near urbanization to bother with a scenic easement.

In the mid-1980s various theories sprang up as to the effects of any nuclear warfare on the livability of the planet. "Starwars" and Ronald Reagan notwithstanding, these were unpredictable times. I sensed a need to find a safe location away from the East Coast to which to migrate should events deteriorate. I was drawn to Western Texas, the High Plains between Midland and EI Paso. Here one could theoretically survive a nuclear winter, given properly constructed shelter and the ability to provide food for oneself. High level wind patterns would minimize any destructive fallout. Sparsity of population would minimize opportunistic scavenging.

After several visits, Louise and I found a beautiful cattle ranch half-way between the towns of Marfa and Alpine in Texas. Twenty-one thousand acres nestled South of two prominent peaks. (These peaks can actually be seen in the movie *Giant* in the two scenes featuring James Dean on his own little spread.) A deal was struck, we purchased the ranch, hired Ken Smith to manage the cattle operation, and went on with our lives. Rather than building a new residence 20 miles from the nearest habitation, we decided to rent an apartment in Alpine. Proximity to shopping and to the airport were important factors. Our pickup truck could provide adequate transportation to and around the ranch whenever needed.

Although at one time I considered placing a scenic easement on the ranch property, the economics mitigated against such a move. The possibility of this land being developed was an event so far into the future, given its location and given the scarcity of water, the present value of the development rights (that which you are giving up by placing the easement) were almost insignificant. In other words, the land by its own nature would basically protect itself.

Now, the cattle operation didn't go as smoothly as anticipated either. We consulted Allan Savory,[2] the guru of Holistic Management techniques, and hoped that his methods would help improve the land. But, sad to say, his methods are just too complicated, involve too many variables, and require day-to-day interventions that most mortals are just not capable of handling. On top of that, we lucked into a bad purchase of calves from Mexico: over half came down with a disease that bore some resemblance to Mad Cow. After several years, the operations were terminated and I decided to resell the property. The good news was that Ronald Reagan had single-handedly prevailed in the Cold War

2 Allan Savory, *Holistic Management* (Island Press, 1998).

and seen to the demise of the Soviet Union, the only really threatening nuclear power in the world.

Not long afterwards, Louise and I divorced. A year or so later I married Pat who had also recently divorced my school and college friend Chas Freeman. Pat was not enamored with the small farm I ended up with in Amherst, so that went back onto the market too. We determined that our best opportunity lay in the renovation of the two farmhouses on the land in Lyme, Connecticut. This project took two years, and, awaiting the completion, we lived temporarily in a neat old house in Old Saybrook: in earlier days it had been an ice house, used to store the winter ice from the adjacent Chalker Pond that was cut to be sold to the railroad for reefer cars. Inside a three-story windowless structure there arose, set at a 45-degree angle to the outer stonewalls, an inner tower with windows and balconies.

By 1994 we were able to move into Brick House, whereupon the Ice House was put on the market. As we settled in, other nearby properties came up for sale. First was a pair of five-acre lots just across the Eight Mile River, owned by the Cooper family, and smack-dab in our view of what had been a pristine natural shoreline. It sat right next to a larger piece of equally beautiful property that the Coopers had earlier donated to the Nature Conservancy. There was no doubt that the proper treatment of the Cooper lots was simply to purchase them, and then immediately protect them with a scenic easement similar to that previously placed on our 271 acre piece. Which we did. The only structure on the Cooper land was a small boathouse near a stone pier on the shore. Later we sold this sliver back to one of the Coopers, as we had no need for the facility.

Next came the opportunity to purchase 30 acres of woodland, with a care-taker's house, from John Barclay. The lot was contiguous to the Western boundary of the 271 acres, North of the Joshua Rock. The flat area at its Southwest corner had previously been grazed, probably by sheep. It had second-growth cedar and black cherry trees intermixed, and was strewn with boulders from the last Ice Age. We approached the DEP again to arrange for another scenic easement. But they were not interested in the formula previously employed, namely permitting only new buildings that were appurtenant to farming. The solution lay in simply cutting out one acre in the Southwest corner from the easement, and then conceding that no new buildings would occupy the remaining 29 acres. Farming, of course, would still be permitted. Starting in 2001 I undertook to clear the flat area, approximately seven acres, to create an additional hay field. All the small stones were buried in a pit 30 feet wide by 120 feet long by 13 feet deep. The biggest boulders were pushed to the edge of the field; a few were later moved to Northpoint's water feature. Eventually, the field was harrowed, fertilized, and seeded with timothy and clover. After several years, the field produced respectably abundant crops of hay.

Then the Jewett Farm along Connecticut Route 156 came on the market. It consisted of over 200 acres straddling the Eight Mile River about a mile North of our home. An eight-acre field lay adjacent to the highway, and had been kept in hay for some time. The property then ascended a steep hill East of the highway, to abut the Nehantic State Forest. Snapped this one right up! The only house, an old Colonial in need of considerable rehabilitation, was sold off with five acres. Then the remainder was subjected to yet another scenic easement, using the same formula as the Barclay piece, namely cutting out one acre to remain unrestricted while preserving building-less the remainder. I later cleared about five more acres, again for hay, down along the Eight Mile River. Spring flooding ensures very productive crops.

CHAPTER XVIII
GOODSPEED AIRPORT

My Tomahawk lived at the Chester Airport, across the Connecticut River. One evening I flew back to Chester to find that the T-hangar I assumed was mine, was occupied by another aircraft. I complained to the management, whose response was, "Oh, just take any available hangar!" Not good enough, I resolved to move across the river to Goodspeed in East Haddam where I knew that a rental would mean specific occupancy of a particular T-hangar. Mrs. Anzalone was the Secretary at Goodspeed, and handled the accounting and gas sales. Once settled in, I asked her if it would be possible to procure a key to the gas pumps so that I could refuel out of hours. She referred me to the owner, Artie DeNoffrio.

Artie runs a propeller repair shop in East Haddam. I visited him, and before long he was explaining to me how it was his intention to actually sell the airport. In fact he was already in negotiations with the Goodspeed Opera House. This piqued my interest because, if I were to purchase it, not only would I be able to make my own set of rules with respect to the sale of fuel, but I had further opportunity to protect yet another beautiful piece of land. The Goodspeed Airport sits right alongside the Connecticut River; its riverfront exceeded 2,100 feet in length. This land, too, had been farmland in prior decades. It became an airport in about 1964, moved from the site subsequently occupied by the Yankee nuclear power plant in Haddam. At the Southern end of this 43-acre parcel sat Chapman Pond, equal in size to the airport, and protected on all sides by unbuildable wetlands. I knew that this airport should eventually be protected from further development.

In June 1999, I purchased the Goodspeed Airport and so no longer had to pay hangar rent to myself. Before long, officials from the Town of East Haddam and the Goodspeed Opera House, which had also been negotiating to purchase the airport, were asking whether or not I would allow the Opera House to use the Northern part of the airport property for additional parking necessary for the expansion of their theater. I developed a plan that would suit their requirements, but asked that as part of the deal the airport be allowed to lengthen the runway and re-orient it clockwise about five degrees. The First Selectman, Susan Merrow (once head of the Sierra Club) asked if this was a *quid pro quo*, and I replied "Yes". Witnessed by my stepson Charles.

Well, negotiations dragged on for some months. A sticking point arose when the East Haddam Land Trust ("EHLT"), which owned a small intervening lot between the Southern end of the airport and Chapman Pond, thought that they should be compensated for going along with the plan, even though I had indicated I was willing to provide them road access to their land which they never had prior. I told them that any additional compensation would have to come from the Opera House, not from me.

I learned from Artie that he had periodically cut trees on the piece of land owned by the EHLT going back to the early 1980s, when he purchased the airport. He memorialized this fact in an Affidavit, which I filed in the Town land records. This gave me the comfort that the airport had a prescriptive easement to keep the trees trimmed so as to maintain safety for pilots landing and taking off over Chapman Pond. In November of that year, I mailed a copy of the Affidavit to the EHLT, then hearing nothing after about a week, I hired Tim Evans to actually cut down the trees on the EHLT land in the area where they had previously been cut. Most were young ailanthus, cedar and locust: nothing to write home about.

The EHLT went into apoplexy. They complained to Jimmy Ventres, the Zoning and Wetlands Enforcement Office in East Haddam (who had earlier told me not to worry about cutting trees so long as the Connecticut Department of Transportation considered it necessary for purposes of aircraft safety). Ventres called a special emergency meeting of the Wetlands Commission (which I just happened to catch on the local community TV channel) and, without inviting the airport (or me) to provide counter testimony, proceeded to resolve to issue a "Cease and Desist" order to the airport for failing to get a wetlands permit before cutting the trees. So much for *due process*!

Now everyone piled on: the East Haddam Land Trust, the Nature Conservancy, the Town of East Haddam, the Connecticut Department of Environmental Protection, as well as the press from Middletown and Hartford. Suits and counter-suits; state and federal courts; lawyers galore; gratuitous interviews and press articles. When the East Haddam Wetlands Commission convened to initiate legal action, we pointed out that three of their five members had conflicts of interest, either for being members of the EHLT or for making prejudicial comments in public venues. The Chairman thereupon closed the meeting, re-opened it in Executive Session, and without a proper quorum including substitutes for the recused members, passed a motion to fine the airport for its trespasses.

Adding insult to injury, they also wanted a remediation plan: restore the plantings that were destroyed. We had to waste money on consultants to develop this plan, but nothing we prepared ever rose to the level that all the opposing parties would sign off on.[1] Settlement discussions

---

1 Interestingly, in the spring of 2000, a pair of bald eagles developed a nest in a tree at the edge of the cleared glide slope. We have a photo of their offspring as proof. Our dastardly tree cutting had actually improved the natural habitat!

came to naught. We essentially decided to leave it up to the judge to obtain the most favorable result.

And Judge Sferrazza came through. He determined that the airport did, in fact, have a prescriptive easement to cut trees on the adjacent property, but that we had exceeded our easement by cutting them to the ground rather than just down to the glide slope prescribed by FAA regulations. He also decided that remediation was not called for since the parties were so far apart on the plan to be implemented. He allowed the Town's fine of $500 per day for 35 days between the cutting and the initiation of legal proceedings. And he allowed the DEP's fine of $50,000, though DEP was not allowed to apply it to remediation, but had to spend it on some nebulously specified research. He granted compensation of $1 to the EHLT because they had not properly evaluated and appraised the damage they claimed. I did send them a check for $1, but to date it has never been cashed.

Attorney General Blumenthal tried to get the airport to pay for his department's legal representation of the DEP. The Connecticut Supreme Court basically told him to go pound sand: those costs were properly part of his job and budget. Don't get me started on Blumenthal. . . . Or on Chris Dodd, for that matter . . . .

Shortly after purchasing the airport my attorney approached the DEP to negotiate a scenic easement on the airport. It contemplated continued use as an airport but allowed for no additional structures or development. Once the tree-cutting anti-airport pogrom commenced, these negotiations could obviously not flourish into any productive conclusion. Nor could they be resuscitated after the lawsuits were finished, because by then I had another conflict with the Town of East Haddam. In 2003, the Airport applied for "Open Space" designation, which granted property tax relief in certain pre-defined zones in the town, including all areas in the flood plain, so long as the parcel's use had not changed for at least fifteen years. The Airport clearly qualified for this tax relief.

Denied. Off to tax court to compel the town to comply with their own regulations. After about eight more years of litigation the Court decided for the Airport. We received a refund in excess of $189,000 for all the years we had been improperly gouged. And from that point in time the property taxes have been reduced by half. Not to mention all the funds the town wasted on such a pointless and impossible quest.

Once the tax litigation was complete, we returned to the DEP to resurrect the scenic easement process. The Connecticut River Gateway Commission, which oversees the special zone of towns that border on the Southern end of the Connecticut River, has heartily endorsed our proposal. In spite of many changes in the upper ranks of the DEP, the organization seems to be yet mired in anti-airport prejudices. Maybe it will have been completed by the time these words are published, in which case I will happily update this paragraph. Meanwhile, my Tomahawk has been sold. We are left with the ongoing maintenance of a beautiful piece of land.

The experience of defending Goodspeed Airport for the sake of maximizing safety to air traffic has just reinforced the lesson learned in my youth. One must stand up for one's beliefs, no matter the odds and the deck stacked against you. The fines I paid to make Goodspeed Airport safe for pilots came to $67,501. Is this worth the price of saving someone from dying unnecessarily in an airplane accident caused by excessively high vegetation on the approach path to the runway? I think so. There has been no fatality at Goodspeed due to the incursion of vegetation into the landing slope in the fifteen years of our stewardship. I intend to keep it that way.

Some people say, "Well, you could afford to spend all that money on lawyers, unlike the average citizen." And that is true, but it misses the basic point: if one is in a position where one's rights are being threatened or attacked, and one *has* the ability to respond, then (it is my firm belief) one has the absolute *obligation* to react in the most forceful and effective manner. As others have said more succinctly, "Freedom is not free."

CHAPTER XIX

WYOMING

There comes a time in one's life when one must take account. What do I mean? We all fall into habits, into ruts, into ways of doing things, into ways of thinking about what is going on around us, what is important, what matters, who are our true friends, and why. I'm not talking about the tipping point between youth and the exuberance manifesting itself in the desire to "do good" and perfect the world, on the one hand, and the more measured consideration of the reality of human nature that dawns on the maturing mind. Churchill said "Show me a young Conservative and I'll show you someone with no heart. Show me an old Liberal and I'll show you someone with no brains."

I have outlined my efforts, proudly supported on the shoulders of many colleagues, to save the New England railroads. No apologies will be forthcoming relative to the course we took to achieve our success. But there is only so much stress that one can endure before one requires respite. And it relates not just to occupation, but also to the whirlwind of social entanglements, including the vicissitudes of family and the external pressures imposed by an ever more complicated world.

For me, the time arrived in 2005. One factor became paramount: we had to remove ourselves from the rat race. Life in Connecticut did not seem satisfactory: too many New Yorkers were moving in, true friends were difficult to make, traffic was becoming alarmingly dangerous, state taxes were always on the increase, the fracas over the airport had become puerile and counter-productive, and life in general was becoming more tense and unpleasant. We decided, therefore, to seek greener pastures.

We explored several alternatives. First, Florida, where we visited both Apalachicola (excellent oysters!) and St. Augustine. Too many people, too many tourists. Then we set out to fly-over country. South Dakota was tax-friendly, but the landscape was boring, boring, boring, even Yankton on the Missouri River. A third journey took us to Wyoming. There we toured by rent-a-car and found promising prospects in the Southeastern quadrant: a beautiful valley South of Casper, the Platte River Valley, and the Laramie Valley. Laramie, with its University of Wyoming, seemed most promising due to the diversity of interests and opportunities.

We called on a realtor in Laramie one morning, James Rheinhart. We knocked on his door, but he was heavily engaged on his cellphone and told us to return in an hour. We did, and prevailed on him to show us some ranch properties in the vicinity. We found two adjacent ranches, the Riverbend and the Mill Iron-S, about 20 miles Southwest of Laramie. Moose grazing along the Laramie River, which bisected both properties, convinced us to buy. The land was not only spectacular, but also highly productive with respect to the cultivation of hay and the grazing of cattle. The deal was sealed by Thanksgiving, and we became citizens of the Great State of Wyoming on the first of December, 2005.

Wyoming is vast. Wyoming is friendly, extra friendly, in fact. Wyoming is peaceful. Driving to Laramie, 19 miles, one might encounter five or six vehicles passing in the opposite direction. But the Laramie Valley is also extremely windy. Pat became agitated by this phenomenon, but gamely pressed on with our new lifestyle. And we were able to return to Connecticut for parts of the year to tend to the gardens and farming activities in the summer.

Our ranch grew as adjoining ranches came up for sale. The X-Bar doubled our acreage. Here again, the penchant to save this beautiful land from future development came to the fore. After other minor consolidations we had accumulated 6,700 acres, sprawling practically seven miles along the length of the Laramie River. Call the appraisers to determine the value of the development rights! We negotiated with the Game and Fish Department of the State of Wyoming to a satisfactory conclusion, and donated these rights to the State for its custody.

Annual visits to my family physician produced ever increasing PSA counts, the lead indicator for the possible presence of prostate cancer. My father had endured the same path, so I became particularly wary. Eventually I was convinced to see a specialist to determine, by biopsy, the extent of the threat. It was real. I opted immediately for laparoscopic surgery to remove the prostate at the hospital in Springfield, Massachusetts. Dr. Agarwal, the surgeon, was from India. He provided great reassurance as to the probability of success, and, after a four and one-half hour procedure, the prostate was gone. The PSA count has been normal (<0.01) ever since.

But the psychological effects of this crisis were not so simple. I felt immediate kinship with Warren Osborne, son of Ernie and Betty Osborne who was claimed by cancer many decades earlier. For what such a predicament presents is the realization that, all of a sudden, you measure your lifespan by what time might remain rather than by some theoretical timespan dictated by the actuaries. I grasped for support that my closest confidants were unable to provide. I had to fight this on my own. I divorced my wife; only to remarry six months later once the crisis had truly passed. We both had learned much about ourselves in the process and vowed to forge ahead into the future with a renewed confidence in our mutual love and sustainability.

On a vacation trip to Iceland and France in the summer of 2008, we developed a new strategy. So as not to have to spend a full half-year in Wyoming, we would purchase an additional residence in a third state, close to Connecticut. Rhode Island seemed perfect due to proximity. Within several weeks of our return, we had located a pair of adjacent lots, both of which were for sale, on the West side of Narragansett Bay. By early November we had closed on both. One had no more than a fisherman's shack, which I reduced to dumpster-size pieces with my backhoe. The other had a contemporary house built in the 1980s. We rehabbed it over the next year. Due to the special beauty of these contiguous eleven acres along the shoreline, we sought, and eventually received, agreement to place yet another scenic easement for its perpetual preservation.

Simultaneously, on the Wyoming front, we set out to find a more manageable (and less windy) ranch to replace the one we had previously assembled. Luck provided the availability of a 1,389 acre spread on the Encampment River near Riverside, just on the Western side of the Snowy Range, in the Platte River Valley.[1] We were able to close this deal by Thanksgiving of the same year, despite horrendously trying and acrimonious negotiations with the Sellers: at the closing we had to occupy separate rooms.

The Flying Diamond Ranch now became ours. Improvements were in order: the plastic Christmas trees along the driveway had to go, as did the sign along the highway advertising their tourist facility; the B&B house of early 20th century vintage was sold to, and hauled eight miles away by a nice young couple that were starting their own life. The main house that had been built by Mr. Horst was in reasonably good condition, but the previous owners had left it in quite messy shape. Now six years later, writing this book in my study in that very house, I can think of no place on Earth more quiet and peaceful and conducive to easy concentration. And we are surrounded by beauty on all sides: the

1 Riverside is in Carbon County. Carbon County is more than seven times the land mass of the entire State of Rhode Island.

pre-Cambrian Baggott rocks to the North, the Encampment River to the East, shrouded in a line of cottonwood trees, and the Sierra Madre Mountains across a valley to the South and West, constituting the Continental Divide that determines whether water flows into the Gulf of Mexico or into the Pacific Ocean.

Rather than sell the original ranch near Laramie, I decided instead on a program that would give it additional use beyond its having been preserved by the scenic easement. I donated the property to the School of Agriculture of the University of Wyoming with the understanding that they could resell it on the open market for no less than the residual price represented by the appraisal used for the scenic easement, and then use the proceeds to fund research efforts in animal diseases such as brucellosis. Such a resale took place several years later.

The Flying Diamond needed its own scenic easement. Piggybacking on the prior success with the Game and Fish Department, we accomplished this in 2010, only two years after our purchase. We retained the right, again, to build structures appurtenant to ranch use within a circle five hundred feet in radius centered on a point roughly in the middle of the small complex of existing ranch buildings.

The following table summarizes the acreage put under these easements over the years:

State	**Property**	**Acreage**
Connecticut	Bross	271
	Cooper	11
	Jewett	195
	Goodspeed	0 (to date)
Rhode Island	Pojac Point	11
Wyoming	Riverbend et.al.	6,700
	Flying Diamond	1,389
		8,577 Total acreage

That is equivalent in aggregate to 13.4 square miles. Not that acreage is everything. What counts most is the quality of the land, in each and every case. "They're not making any more of it," after all.

CHAPTER XX
NORWAY

Norway I consider to be my second country. I was told long ago (I can't remember by whom) that my Conover grandparents were part Norwegian. Ever since I visited Norway with my father in 1956, fishing for salmon in the Stryn River at the East end of the Nordfjord, I have been enamored of the place. The people are hearty, and for the most part of excellent temperament. The scenery is majestic. The climate is tolerable and only in the dead of winter, when the sun rises above the horizon for less than four hours each day, do people there become slightly subdued.

In the summer of 1960, my then-*fiancée* Sue studied at the National University in Oslo. After we were married in 1963, she proposed that we both return to tour the country by car. So in May of 1964, we rented a VW bug in Stavanger and threaded our way Northward along the various fjords and through the intervening mountains, ending up in Älesund. We passed through Stryn, where I had been fishing. The snowdrifts on the pass at Grotli were twice the height of our car, still in May. We passed the beautiful Geiranger Fjord and descended the Trolsweg (hairpin turn after hairpin turn) in a blizzard. In those days many of the roads were only one lane wide, with periodic passing areas. Luckily, the traffic was correspondingly light.

One of the amazing sights on this trip was the stave church in the hamlet of Borgund, just East of Lærdal at the head of the Sognfjord. Built in the 13th century, this iconic wood structure symbolized the transition of the indigenous population from Paganism to Christianity. There used to be hundreds of similar stave churches throughout Scandinavia. Today, only 27 or so have survived. I would revisit this place years later.

I have returned to the fishing camp in Stryn several times. First in 1992 with Dieter and his wife Lynette and the Jacksons to fish for salmon; then in 1993 on my honeymoon with Pat, but not to fish, just to climb the boggy mountainside and enjoy the autumn views. Hans, my gillie in 1956, visited us and wanted not the delicious Aquavit we offered, but simply a Coke. He remembered trolling the river with me in the evening sessions and the 18 pounder I caught with a prawn as bait.

Figure 14: Original Borgund Stave Church.

The third visit to Stryn came many years later. I had been studying various reference books about wooden Norwegian structures. The *loft* was a storage building typical on many small Norwegian farms: it was used to store grains through the winter, then acted as sort of a guest house during the summer. Built on stilts approximately a meter high, the structure was designed defensively against the invasion of rats. Huge logs formed an enclosed square, with only a single door to gain access. A second story, cantilevered out on three or four sides and accessible by a very steep set of stairs, sat atop. A pitched roof, usually of sod, and often adorned with a dragon carving, covered the structure. Wouldn't it be neat, I thought, to recreate one of these *lofts*?

David Miller, the skilled restorer who rebuilt our two farmhouses in Lyme in 1993-4, had to be convinced to take on such a complicated task. We wooed him into considering it by offering to take him to Norway to look at several of these *lofts*. Joyce, his wife, came along. The lure of salmon fishing at the end of the trip was too much for these two avid anglers to pass up. So off we flew to Nottoden in the Southern county of Telemark. On the approach, I could actually see the *loft* at Heddal that I had studied in so many reference books. We drove there immediately and were greeted by the Torgersons. They graciously agreed to allow us to come the following morning to take pictures of their historic Havsten *loft*. David took many rolls of film, from which he was able to determine all the joinery necessary to recreate our own version. We set out to visit other *lofts* in the area, but found none so beautiful as the Havsten *loft*. Then we drove Northward to Stryn to enjoy the week of salmon fishing that we had offered as bait. David caught the only sizable salmon, as apparently the Swedes who annually rented the camp at the beginning of the season had practically fished the river clean.

Figure 15: Havsten Loft in Heddal Norway.

You don't find logs such as these at Home Depot. Made of pine, the logs necessary to construct such a *loft* had to be 32 inches in diameter, and as straight as possible with no crooks, rot or splits. We lucked into finding a grove of such trees in East Haddam, just North of our home in Lyme. Mr. Cone, the owner was amenable to selling us 35 trees on the stump. But tradition dictated that they couldn't just be chopped down: rather, they had to be topped (removing the top 20 percent, which included most of the leafy part), then let stand for over a year so that the sap could be forced out from between the grains by the natural spring flowing process. Perma Treat then harvested the small crop and transported the logs to Lyme.

We purchased a Woodmizer sawmill from the Estate of Gus Carlson (my former colleague at Insulating Shade who had unfortunately just passed away) and David began the process of debarking, then shaping the pine logs. Each had to be turned from a rounded cross-section to an ovoid cross-section, which gave each log the appearance of being of greater diameter than it actually was. Flat stone boulders in a 3x3 matrix formed the base of the structure. Atop these lay three parallel beams, which were in turn fitted with the meter-long spiders at the intersections. Then the main cross beams set atop the spiders.

The tricky part was the construction of the sides of the first story out of the aforementioned shaped logs: since logs are naturally tapered, the tip end of one log had to match up with the butt end of the log beneath. Then each had to be notched at each end to accommodate the junction with the two logs on the adjoining side. Each log then had four notches. And not just any old notch: the notches had to be cut just as they had been traditionally in Scandinavia. Furthermore, the biggest diameter logs had to be at the bottom, with smaller and smaller logs fitted as they progressed upwards. David is a very patient, and very talented craftsman. He also had to create a keyway on the bottom of each log that would accommodate the rounded top of the log below. Once the building was finished, one could detect from the inside of this lower room (once the door was closed) not a single ray of outside light. Absolute perfection.

Rounded posts functioned as corners for the enclosed balcony of the upper story. These were carved into a fluted shape by David. Other carvings adorned the several apertures, and the post that topped the front of the structure. We celebrated the completion of the loft on the 17th of May (Norwegian National Day) in 2008 and hosted a dinner under tent adjacent to the lighted *loft*. The Torgersons came all the way from Norway. We toasted the craftsmen, whose four years of toil had culminated in this beautiful re-creation. We consumed vast quantities of gravlax, the traditional marinated salmon, along with copious amounts of Aquavit.

David's woodworking shop was in the top of my old barn. One day shortly before the completion of the *loft* I happened in for a purpose that now escapes me. There, nailed to the wall, was a picture of a stave church. Annotated in magic marker with the exclamation "NEXT?!"

Figure 16: Our loft in Lyme.

LOL, as the texters taunt. It took very little time to accede to this brazen dare: the answer being, "You're on!" Second trip to Norway to canvas the possibility of actually building a Stave church. This time we landed in Bergen, rented a car, and visited the four most promising examples: Vik, Borgund, Kaupanger and Ulnes, all more or less situated around the Sognefjord. The church at Borgund (which I had first visited in 1964) proved to be the best candidate. Its proportions and lines were exquisite and it happened to be of a size that just fit the maximum dimensions permitted by the Zoning Regulations from the Town of Lyme.

The most favorable site for this Borgund replica would be in that one acre carved out from the scenic easement on the property previously purchased from Mr. Barclay. This site is in the Southwest corner of the hay field I had cleared, the highest area on a gently sloping triangular field. Since in no way could this replica be compromised to accommodate modern building codes, such as the need for handicap ramps at each entry, or lavatories for occupants, I had to sell the project to the Zoning Officer as being a "sculpture" rather than a building. He was convinced, and so signed a building permit.

Unlike the original, our church is built atop a full cellar in order to accommodate mechanical functions such as electric service and alarm systems. Additionally, the cellar protects the wooden upper structure from ground moisture. Perma Treat found the stands of pine suitable for the pieces we needed to cut and shape. The same sawmill as used on the *loft* was pressed back into service. The upright staves, 14 in number, had to be absolutely straight and at least 26 feet in length. During the winter months, when the weather precluded working outside, David and his son Stephen formed and carved the St. Andrews crosses that adorn the interior superstructure, as well as the figureheads at the upper end of each stave.

"Who was the architect?" someone asked. The truth is: there was no architect. The Norwegians would not provide us plans that had been drawn from the original. So David reverse-engineered the entire structure from the 900 photographs that he and Joyce had snapped while in Norway. The many reference books on the subject of stave churches were also very helpful. The nave gradually arose from the main floor structure. Simultaneously, a stone walkway was built around the entire outside to accommodate the ambulatory. The outline of the chancel followed the nave, and finally the apse.

The staves were connected at various upper levels by cross-beams. These had to be fortified with wooden "knees", whole pieces of wood forming a 90-degree curve and formed from the arc between the bottom of the tree trunk and the main outspreading roots. Most of these came from Nova Scotia and were carved from tamarack trees. Pat and I hauled them back on my 16-foot trailer, across the Bay of Fundy on a ferry, and down through Maine. We had a difficult few hours at US Customs, as apparently new regulations had just gone into effect limiting the importation of certain Canadian woods due to beetle infestations. Fortunately, our import fell within the three-month warning-only grace period!

Tapered shingles were also procured from afar. Made of Arctic cedar, they had to be pre-cut to various sizes and transported to Connecticut from Northern Wisconsin. We needed more than 28,000 shingles to finish both the roofs and many of the exterior vertical surfaces. Gary Gustafson, the master shingler, did a magnificent job both shaping each individual shingle (they came to a point, somewhat like fish scales), and applying them to each surface.

Our goal was to complete the church in time to hold another celebration on the 17th of May in 2014. The remaining steps involved a creative landscaping scheme, produced by our friend Anne Vaterlaus, and implemented by Phil Trowbridge, a local masonry contractor. The implementation became a huge problem and headache: Trowbridge had been ordering his cut stone from a supplier near Binghamton, New York. Poor winter weather and even poorer business practices led to delay after delay. Much of the finished design had to be fudged to make the scene presentable for the party, which itself went off without a hitch. Months after the party, the full landscape design came to complete fruition. The final result is breath-taking in its beauty. Tom Delaney's magnificent drone video (vimeo.com/113116784 - no longer available) highlights the beauty.

Figure 17: Our Borgund Stave Church.

What will be the use for this iconic triumph? Our Borgund stave church will likely never be used as a place of worship: in order to keep the result as exactly reflective of the original structure in Norway, the building could not meet standard contemporary building codes. Therefore, it cannot be "occupied" in the normal sense of the word. It can, however, be admired as a sculpture and as a representation of a cultural phenomenon of centuries past. Though not now associated with any formal religion, this Borgund artifact is nonetheless a very spiritual place; a place where one can come to enjoy peace and solitude; a venue for contemplation.

CHAPTER XXI

TIGHAR HUNT

One day in March 2012, I was sitting in my office at home in Wyoming, just where I am sitting now as I write. Pat returned from shopping in Saratoga and, handing me a copy of the Casper Star Tribune, said, "I thought you might be interested in this article about Amelia Earhart." My wife still rues that day.

Amelia Earhart was the famous aviatrix who attempted to be the first female pilot to circumnavigate the globe in 1937. My own particular interest stems from the coincidence that Earhart was involved in the formation of Boston Maine Airways several years earlier. The original Boston Maine Airways was a joint venture between the Boston and Maine Railroad and the Maine Central Railway. The impetus stemmed from the fierce competition between railroads in those years to provide the fastest service for both passengers and mail. Of course, these very same two railroads are the ones we conjoined in the early 1980s when we formed Guilford Transportation Industries.

Additionally, and equally coincidental, Boston Maine Airways had contracted with Pan American Airways to form an airmail route from Boston Northward through Maine to Portland and Bangor. The fact that we purchased the second iteration of Pan Am out of bankruptcy in 1998, and based the new Pan Am at Pease International Airport in Portsmouth, New Hampshire just flavors the coincidence. And none of this has anything to do with a third coincidence, namely that I attended Yale University and graduated in 1964, the same year as my friend Ed Trippe, the son of Juan Trippe, the original organizer of Pan American Airways.

The article in the Casper paper described a news conference at the US Department of State at which Secretary of State Hillary Clinton and Secretary of Transportation Ray LaHood were touting the proposed expedition to the South Pacific to further investigate the Earhart disappearance in 1937. They called attention to the forensic analysis performed by Jeff Glickman to a photograph of what was thought might be part of a landing gear protruding from the surf in a picture taken only several months after the Earhart disappearance.

Glickman was working for an organization named The International Group for Historic Aircraft Recovery, better known as "TIGHAR". Founded by Ric Gillespie, a former aviation insurance adjuster, TIGHAR had since its inception in 1982 made over ten expeditions to the tiny atoll named Nikumaroro, which lay several hundred miles South of the Equator in what is now the territory belonging to Kiribati. Gillespie had built a name for his organization by finding not only artifacts that arguably could have belonged to castaways who might have inhabited Niku. He also relied heavily on a written transcript by Betty, a Florida schoolgirl who was fond of listening to short wave radio, of transmissions which she believed came from Amelia Earhart and her navigator Fred Noonan on the days just after the disappearance. Betty kept a notebook and tried as best she could to record the sentences she heard. Particular references to numbers such as "337/157" and "271 miles North" suggested authenticity when compared to radio transmission from Earhart to the Coast Guard ship Itasca as she approached her intended destination of Howland Island just North of the Equator. Having never found Howland, the theory developed, she searched for an alternate landing spot and ended up on the reef on the Northwest corner of Nikumaroro.

TIGHAR's Gillespie announced at this Department of State event that he was now planning yet another expedition to the same atoll, "Niku VII", to search for the Earhart aircraft in the vicinity of the alleged landing gear in the 1937 photo. He claimed that State Department analysts had corroborated Glickman's evaluation. (However, subsequent emails produced under the Freedom of Information Act shows this not to be the case.) The area could easily be recognized because the same photo had captured the wreck of the steamship Norwich City which had fetched up on the reef in 1929 as the result of a horrendous storm. It had been hauling lumber between Vancouver and New Zealand; eleven sailors lost their lives, but the New Zealand Navy was able to rescue the remainder.

TIGHAR, a non-profit 501(c)(3) organization based in Delaware, was seeking donations to fund Niku VII. The budget exceeded two million dollars, and contemplated renting the research vessel *Ka'imikai-o-Kanaloa* ("K-o-K") from the University of Hawaii, sailing 1800 miles to Nikumaroro and back, and spending ten days on site deploying side-scan sonar using an Autonomous Underwater Vehicle ("AUV") and a Remotely Operated Vehicle ("ROV") with high definition cameras to find the hapless Lockheed 10E Electra on the underwater slope of the atoll.

Because of my companies' connections with Amelia Earhart, because of my interests in aviation and my own world circumnavigations, and because this strange mystery seemed (from what little I knew at the time) so close to solution, I decided that my support would be a useful contribution. I phoned Gillespie and expressed my interest in making a donation. He had already received various corporate commitments from Lockheed, The Discovery Channel, and FedEx, amounting in aggregate to about $600,000. How much was I thinking of chipping in, asked Gillespie. I told him I would be willing to donate one half of the budget. This was enough to allow him to signal "GO" to the participants even though he had not garnered commitments for the full amount.

Such a significant donation meant that I would be allowed to participate, if I chose to do so. Which I did. On the first of July, 2010, I flew to Honolulu on Hawaiian Airlines (excellent service, good food) and took my place aboard ship. Delayed a day for the arrival of the Kiribati customs officer, Sam, the ship sailed on the 3rd. Nine uneventful days later we arrived at Nikumaroro. Others have better described this God-forsaken atoll, but to put it politely, it's not exactly what you would call a Tourist Destination. July, ("winter" South of the Equator) and daily temperatures approach 115 degrees Fahrenheit. The beaches are polluted with ghastly amounts of trash, especially plastic water bottles and those rubbery flip-flops. Sharks everywhere, even in the shallow lagoon around which the atoll stretches. Save for one afternoon's excursion on shore, we choose to remain aboard ship for the entire stay.

TIGHAR had contracted with Phoenix International to actually perform the search operations. Phoenix had just recently been successful in finding the remains of the doomed Air France flight in the South Atlantic. But Phoenix's efforts were flawed. They first deployed the AUV to map the entire underwater area adjacent to the suspected landing area used by Earhart. But the AUV was not properly programmed: it went downhill easily enough, but when it was turned to come back uphill, it could not make the grade, so it ran into the cliff, twice getting stuck. The algorithm was changed to only take sonar pictures on the way down, which meant twice as much time to cover a given area. When the AUV got stuck, it had to be rescued by the ROV. This became a very tense operation because the ROV was controlled through a tether, and the tether was only just long enough to reach the depth of the AUV. The ROV had a claw and, once found, the AUV was snatched and pulled backwards out of the cliff-side cave. All in all, these diversions cost valuable time.

Once the side-scan sonar data had been processed, we could look for what seemed to be promising targets. Using the ROV and its Standard

Definition real-time video, each target was examined up close. Most turned out to be just boulders. One target appeared to me to take the shape of an aircraft wing, tapered at one end, and consisting of about fifteen parallel ribs fore and aft. When approached by the ROV, however, it became obvious that we were looking at either a hatch cover or a bulkhead from the wreck of the Norwich City. And, naturally, it lay exactly down-slope from the shipwreck on the reef, amongst a huge pile of bent steel that had once made up the stern section of the ship.

I urged Ric to abandon the AUV part of the strategy and concentrate instead on the video capabilities of the ROV in the area he thought most likely to contain aircraft wreckage, namely down-slope from the presumed position of that landing gear (referred to by TIGHAR as "the Bevington Object" and named for the photographer who took the picture in late 1937). We had already wasted four of the nine days allotted to research. Heated arguments with Phoenix ensued, but Ric prevailed and the ROV became the center of attention.

Wolfgang Burnside, a crusty Scotsman, owned and operated the ROV. He controlled the ROV from inside a freight container that had been bolted down to the top deck of the K-o-K. Ric occupied a seat just to his right, so that both had a view of the monitor that displayed the real time images from the ROV. Wolfgang deftly maneuvered the ROV down the steep slopes on the Northwestern end of the atoll, using a predetermined pattern, up and down, that was referred to as "mowing the lawn". The ROV could descend to about 2000 feet below sea level all the while taking video, both standard and high definition, that was recorded top-side. Only the standard definition could be seen in real time, however, due to bandwidth limited by the tether. High Definition video required computer processing that had to await Mark Smith's return to New Jersey for compilation.

On the very first ROV excursion, glimpses were caught of a section of rope. One problem became immediately apparent: there was no means of determining the size of an object such as a rope because the ROV lacked any device to demonstrate scale. I learned later that two parallel laser beams, 50 millimeters apart, was the standard method of placing scale into the video. Why nobody thought to bring this along is very mysterious, being that all involved purported to be expert in underwater search and recovery. Later, I did come to the conclusion that scale was, in fact, available then and there: the ROV's claw, of known dimension, could have been extended to touch any object of interest.

On the previous expedition, Niku VI in 2010, a similar rope had been found extending up and down the slope in roughly the same area as this first 2012 ROV dive. Along with a loop of what looked like wire, these two artifacts had been memorialized on YouTube in January of 2012 in a two and a quarter minute compilation from the 2010 quasi-High Definition video.[1] But not much attention was paid to this coincidence. The remaining ROV dives in 2012 produced little additional evidence of things man-made, save for a few bottles here and there that could have been jettisoned by just about anyone.

Having exhausted our allotted time on station, we steamed back to Honolulu, pretty much empty handed. On the return trip, Ric Gillespie was able to examine the Standard Definition video in greater detail and more at leisure. There was one area, fairly close to the surface (ascertained by the depth indicator embedded in the video itself), that appeared to contain a smoothly formed surface with straight edges. We pondered the possibility of it being an elevator from the plane. Wolfgang dashed our hopes when he insisted that it could be nothing more than an area of sand.

1 See: https://www.youtube.com/watch?v=P9NXJnwJmRY

CHAPTER XXII

TIGHAR VIDEOS

Once settled in back home, I had occasion to tune into the TIGHAR website to follow up on whatever new information could be gleaned from the videos taken during Niku VII. Jeff Glickman had been tasked with reviewing the High Definition videos to determine if anything not seen in real time could be considered as evidence of an airplane. Along about October, under pressure from the Discovery Channel that had negotiated the exclusive rights to record the expedition and any discoveries thereto related, Glickman identified about a two-minute clip, from shallow waters, with several frames in which four or five yellow arrows pointed to objects that were conceivably connected. As hard as I looked at them, I could not convince myself.

Meantime, I discovered the TIGHAR Forum, where interested folks could comment on various topics related to the disappearance of Earhart, Noonan and their Electra. I had not known about the Forum before the Niku VII Expedition. I was surprised when I discovered that a certain thread started in January of the same year had become a discussion of the various aspects of the short High Definition video spliced together from the 2010 Niku VI expedition. When I say spliced, I mean that time-stamps on each of the frames (30 per second) showed that the second half of the video occurred in real time before the first half. The video concentrated on the "Wire and Rope" artifacts, previously described.

Sometime in late August, John Balderston, who was an employee of Lockheed Martin, posted a picture of what he thought was a painted numeral "2" on the outer edge of what might have been the right wing of the Electra. And not far away, though not properly aligned, a numeral "0". To me it certainly looked more plausible than the items that were soon to be identified by Glickman. I started to examine this video more carefully. The more I looked, the more items I thought I could discern: things like the tail wheel, the cockpit and pilot's seat, a pair of binoculars (known to be aboard the aircraft from the inventory taken after the accident at Luke Field in Hawaii earlier in 1937), and a main landing gear with collapsed tire. I took screen shots of these items and started to accumulate them on a new thread opened for that purpose.

Ric Gillespie could not agree that anything I identified was anything but chance shapes of coral. Many others on the Forum agreed with him, though John Balderston maintained an approach similar to mine and kept identifying aircraft features from the same areas shown in the video. Since only just over two minutes of video had been posted, I asked Gillespie if he would provide a longer, and continuous, stretch of film that included both of the parts already posted. He complied with an eight minute 33 second segment. This, in turn, allowed me to identify yet more aircraft components, as well as shapes that I thought might be the heads of the two crewmembers encased in cellophane bags, with gas bubbles confined. Could the two have used nitrogen from the bottles accompanying the aircraft for inflating the landing gear struts to do themselves in when they realized their predicament was hopeless?

Doubt from other Forum members, especially Gillespie, turned to incredulity, followed not long after by outright scorn and derision. I was offered the opportunity to visit Glickman, TIGHAR's unpaid volunteer forensic expert, at his place near Seattle. If I could convince Glickman that anything I saw was related to Earhart, then they would have to agree. Glickman, though politely hospitable, reviewed my exhibits but could not reach agreement with me on even one item. I went back to the rope, which had been identified earlier by others. It had a peculiar metal fixture on the lower end that bent into the underlying slope. I opined that it might be either part of the radio antenna which spanned the length of the Electra from the cabin to the tail, or perhaps a tie-down rope used to secure the aircraft when parked on the ground. No, Glickman insisted, that rope was a fishing line dropped from a trawler. I challenged him to go on the internet and find a fishing hook shaped anywhere near comparable to the fixture that was attached to the rope in the video. He demurred.

Glickman, using his fancy suite of computer equipment, showed me another version of the videos than those I had been assuming were the ultimate available in terms of clarity. His were twice as clear because there were twice as many pixels in each dimension. "How do I get hold of this?" I asked? Talk to Ric. When I did pose the question, Ric agreed to provide the Highest Definition available, but warned that I would need an especially powerful computer to view it. OK, I'll get one. Ric claimed this quality was only necessary for the folks making the documentaries at the Discovery Channel, and that one really couldn't see anything more in them than the lesser version.

What bunk. The Extra High Definition, as I called them, revealed yet additional features heretofore unrecognizable. And bear in mind, these films were all from 2010, not from the 2012 expedition which I accompanied. That led me to plead for the Extra High Definition videos from 2012. When made available, I found that I was discovering whole new areas with even more relevant artifacts. Mark Smith provided sixteen minutes. I asked for more on either side. Then Ric's patience snapped. No more video footage. Worse, no more posting of alleged aircraft components on his Forum. He took the adamant position that whatever I was posting was pure conjecture, and thus making a mockery of his supposedly scientific approach to research that had given TIGHAR its initial credibility.

The most irksome criticism came in the form of a complaint that nothing I posted was verifiably what I claimed because there was NO SCALE! Well, duh, now who's fault was that? Neither 2010 nor 2012 ROVs sported the simple laser system described earlier. That system had been available in 2010 according to the Seabotix expert who went along to operate the ROV. And at no additional charge to TIGHAR! Surely, if it was available in 2010, it could also have been made available by Wolfgang Burnside in 2012. Something smelled fishy here.

I decided to hire my own forensic analysts to examine the video footage in question. I needed to determine if new and independent eyes could see things that I could see, whether there were ways to measure them reliably in such a way at to be able to compare them with parts from actual existing Electra aircraft, and thereby come to some conclusion about the actual probability of the Earhart Electra being where I had become to believe it was. Dr. John Jarrell from Rhode Island went straight away to work. Within a few short months his firm was able to muster enough data and accompanying graphics to make a strong case in the affirmative. He concentrated on the tail-wheel and the main landing gear that I had identified because of the large number of video frames, from different angles, that could be analyzed as a collection.

Figure 18, right, is an example of debris I consider most likely part of Amelia Earhart's Electra. I believe this shows the underside of the left wingtip of her aircraft. This shot comes from the High Definition Video taken in 2012, obtained through discovery. The depth is approximately 1050 feet, and the location is off the Northwestern tip of the Nikumaroro atoll.

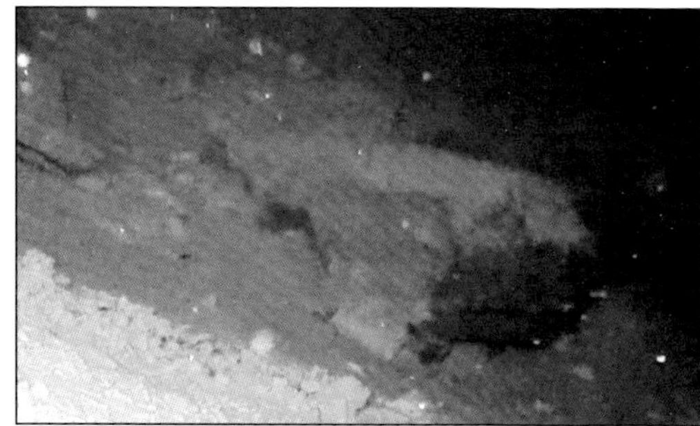

Figure 18: Wingtip from NR16020.

CHAPTER XXIII

TIGHAR STRIPES

What was bugging me, I think, was the reluctance shown by Ric Gillespie to any notion that appeared to advance the quest of actually finding and identifying the Earhart Electra. Gillespie had started this saga as early as 1982. On earlier expeditions, all efforts were directed towards combing the atoll for evidence of a castaway existence. Much was made of some shoe heels that were found on the middle 1990s at what was supposedly a camp site at the opposite (Southeast) end of the atoll. Also a sextant box. And a jar of what was determined to be freckle cream. Amelia had freckles.

Searching underwater for the aircraft did not commence until 2010, more than a quarter century after Gillespie's initial hunch, and in spite of the plethora of valuable hints as to the whereabouts of the landing that were gleaned from Betty and her notebook. The 2010 ROV search was a semi-fiasco in itself: the ROV cable used to control the vehicle was severally damaged by the boat's propeller; the GPS position verification was faulty and could not be relied upon to go back to a "known" position. Then, with hours of High Definition video produced, none of it seemed to have been analyzed with much care or interest. The small YouTube piece was not even posted for interested TIGHAR members to see or analyze for over a year and a half after the completion of the 2010 expedition. When finally interested Forum members commented on this or that, their comments would be countered with Ric's derision, designed to humiliate and quash further attempts. A piece of black cord that very much resembles electric wires to a headset was dismissed as being nothing more than some sort of gasket material from a ship. So informed of this was Ric, by a member of the boat's crew.

More problems surfaced in 2012 (as if what I have already described weren't enough). The ROV had two cameras attached: the Standard Definition camera to take the real-time video could be swiveled in place so that the ROV at rest on the bottom could pan the scenery right to left, up and down; the un-panable High Definition camera was attached at a different part of the ROV. Unfortunately, its angle differed quite drastically from that of the SD camera, such that when the ROV was descending the steep slope and appearing straight ahead at visible terrain, the HD camera was pointed (relatively) upward, and often captured nothing but expanses of empty water, peppered with flakes of falling talus. A good minute of SD footage, which I believe shows pieces of pushrod valves from one of the Electra engines, has comparable HD footage showing . . . NOTHING!

And why in the world terminate discussion about possible airplane parts? If they were actually there, Ric Gillespie's multi-decade effort would be finally vindicated. He could return to fetch a piece or two to convince the most dubious of critics, proclaim victory, and go on to the next aviation mystery. If nothing I saw was anything but a mirage, then he would be no further ahead, but also no further behind. What other motive could come to bear that would explain such ostrich-like behavior?

Follow the money! I've heard that adage before. But in the case of TIGHAR I thought it might just be good advice. TIGHAR's books are not open to the public. Yet I knew, from my own experience with our Sachem Fund, that every non-profit must file an annual report (Form 990) disclosing some basic financial and personnel information for the prior fiscal year. In May 2013, when the last filing extension had finally lapsed, I demanded to see TIGHAR's 990 for the year July 2011 through June 2012. Much resistance to providing the 990 came back my way. But since anyone from the public is entitled to review this form, I knew that he would eventually have to fork it over. Which he did.

In the fiscal year 2011-2012, TIGHAR had revenues (mostly contributions) totaling $1,958,333. This included my gift of stock in April, worth $1,054,459. Gillespie's salary that year was $186,336, not that modest for such a small non-profit organization. The following year, which included the Niku VII expedition and its aftermath, revenues slipped to $257,126. Yet Ric's salary jumped 28 percent to $238,500 (or 92.7 percent of revenues for that year). This in spite of a $430,000 shortfall in fundraising to cover the expenses of the Niku VII expedition. Mr. Berwind, a Director, apparently stepped in to loan TIGHAR the shortfall, and we know that as of early 2014 none of it has been paid back.

I believe that pocketing 92.7 percent of revenues for the Executive Director's salary is unconscionable for an organization of this size and importance. TIGHAR is no more than a cash cow to support the Gillespie lifestyle and aura. These figures led me to conclude that the motive in play here has not been to actually find the Earhart Electra, but rather to perpetuate the search for as many years as possible in order to maintain the lifestyle to which the Gillespies have become accustomed. And it's not just the salary. Consider that a trip to the South Pacific every two years is an expected "duty" of his office. Consider that fancy dining in Philadelphia, at Members' expense, is also a necessary duty for fundraising purposes. I have filed a Form 13909 Tax-Exempt Organization Complaint to the Internal Revenue Service describing certain of these abuses and requesting their determination as to whether private inurement or excess benefit transactions have taken place.

"A tiger doesn't change his stripes . . . ." That is why, in the late Spring of 2013, I brought suit against TIGHAR and against Richard Gillespie in the US District Court in Casper, Wyoming claiming Fraud, Negligent Misrepresentation, RICO and Negligence. The suit is now in Appeal.

CHAPTER XXIV
COLLECTOR

Many people fancy themselves as collectors. Art in the form of painting or sculpture seems to come to mind. Some like to collect stamps. Or vintage automobiles. Or bottle caps. My own tendency has always been a desire to collect skills, or the practical knowledge and experience of doing things.

Maybe this urge started when I was about four and I learned how to put together those electric trains. It wasn't the running of the trains around the track that interested me so much as coming up with challenging track layouts, figuring out the various electrical connections, keeping the equipment in good shape and knowing how to fix things when they broke.

In my early teens I had the opportunity to learn some farming skills. I have described being charged with mowing, raking and transporting hay. In later life I was able to build upon these skills when I started in 1997, or so, to make my own hay in Lyme. I began with the few small fields around our house, with used haying equipment purchased from Kahn Tractor: a Haybine (mower), rake, and baler. First year's product was not of high quality. The hay once cut should have had more time to dry, and the baler tension was improperly set too loose so that each bale weighed no more than about 25 pounds. Live and learn.

In subsequent years I added the Jewett fields along Route 156, and eventually the area surrounding the runway at Goodspeed Airport. Production ramped up over the years to over 1200 bales. The challenge became the selling of the hay rather than its production. Not only did the quality have to be superior in order to satisfy fussy horse owners, but the delivery had to be coordinated with their schedules and also with the weather. Except for loading the hay trailers, which required additional manpower, I performed all these functions just by myself. Included was the maintenance of the hay equipment such as periodic greasing and replacing damaged blades on the sickle bar of the mower.

Now, I must admit to never having developed any particular skill in sports. Team sports, in particular, held very little interest for me. While at Fenn School I was able to become semi-proficient in riflery; the range was in the basement of Robb Hall, beneath the large Assembly room. My tennis game improved over the years, but my skill levels were way less than optimum. I also enjoyed swimming. Skiing came along later, after college, and I have gradually improved to what I would call an "Intermediate+" level. I stopped skiing in 2011 due to my decreasing energy level that eventually evidenced itself in a heart attack in 2013. (Appendix B contains my medical history.) But now after rehab and daily exercise regimens, I feel well enough to resume. I think I will stick to the easier slopes, nonetheless.

One valuable talent I learned at Milton Academy was waiting and bussing dining room tables. Each table had twelve seats. I prided myself on being able to pick up, scrape, and accumulate all twelve main course plates on my extended left arm. Don't try this at home, or your wife may have a fit.

Another skill, described earlier, involved the programming of computers. From my first efforts at Yale, through the experience of developing quite complicated control systems for the IBM 1130 computer group, I would consider this skill to be one of the hardest to master. It is not all that difficult to write a computer program, even one that works properly in all instances. Where higher levels of skill are required are those situations where some aspect of the available resources must be optimized. This could be either the speed at which the program performs its task, or the size of the program if internal processing space is limited, or the eloquence of the appearance of the "output" (numeric and/or graphic).

When we started Perma Treat it was my job (amongst others) to manage the company's finances. The year 1977 was the heyday of the desktop, its DOS operating system, and the stand-alone processing not linked to other computer users. I had to develop the various programs that handled payroll, general ledger, sales invoicing, inventory control and purchasing. BASIC was the name of the language most commonly in use for these small computers. C-BASIC was a variant that I found more useful because of its extended capabilities.

The point I wish to emphasize is the absolute necessity that such programs had to work perfectly before they were put into general use. Making an error in the production of a payroll check is not an acceptable outcome: an angry employee is bad enough, but mistakes that lead to IRS audits or, worse, charges of fraud, can devastate a company in short order. Although my computer programming career lasted no more than about 20 years, I felt that I had mastered the skill to a point of considering myself professional. The skill is generally not one easily forgotten, and I would be able to bank on my familiarity with the processes for decades in other lines of endeavor. Sweet-talking IBM salesmen, for example, could not convince our railroads to purchase systems that were second-rate compared to those of their competitors.

Perma Treat was also the petri dish for my education into the arcane field of accounting. I knew nothing about accounting when we started; I had never heard of double-entry bookkeeping. One day I was visiting Cooke's Equipment in Wallingford, arranging for the purchase of our Massey Ferguson front-end loader. I asked their accountant, who happened to be George Cooke's sister, how I should properly book the entries for this transaction. She sat down with me for about an hour and patiently went through the explanations of each line item required to reflect the purchase: cash, assets, sales tax, accounts payable and so forth. By the time I left I had sufficient familiarity that I was able to design, create, maintain, and use a General Ledger system on our small computer. I still use the same system now, thirty-seven years later.

Speaking of the Massey Ferguson, Perma Treat also provided me with the opportunity to operate a front-end loader. We purchased the machine as a tool to move railroad ties, sawdust and chips around our plant's yard. It also proved useful in the actual construction of our manufacturing facility. I found a large natural deposit of sand near the PT entry gate and used it to line the bottom of the trench we had dug along Air Line Drive for the burial of the power and telephone cables.

I also tried my hand at operating the log grapple on the back of our International Harvester log truck. Finished railroad ties had to be transferred into gondola cars for transport to our customer (say Conrail, or Amtrak). Once treated with creosote, those railroad ties can be slippery little devils; I decided that this particular skill should be left to those way more proficient than me.

Many years later, on our farm in Lyme, I became adept at the use of a backhoe. My small Kubota came with a backhoe that I used to clear and enlarge the fields. I would dig around the periphery to sever the roots from the trunk, then use the arm to push the tree all the way over. Finally, cutting the trunk into pieces (12-inch minimum tip for a railroad tie), pushing the slash onto a large pile for grinding into mulch, and stacking the logs were all part of the process.

One time, I felled a black birch. I grasped the butt end with the claw of the backhoe: I cut off the stump then attacked the next nine bottom feet. What I didn't realize was that the emergency brake on the Kubota had slipped off; thereby creating downhill tension on the section I was about to remove. When the cut was complete, the uphill portion snapped back and fell onto my leg, breaking both lower bones. A lesson learned in SAFETY, the hard way. Dr. Miller at Lawrence and Memorial Hospital fixed me up with an eleven-millimeter titanium rod inserted into the center of the Fibula.

A more robust backhoe was in order. I purchased a John Deere 310E when it came time to clear the seven acre field on which the church was eventually sited. The "E" stood for "extend" and referred to the outer arm of the backhoe which, by separate foot control, telescoped out an additional three or four feet. Turns out this function is the most powerful of those available to the operator, and found its greatest use when it was time to push a tree over. Some years later, after the field had been hayed a few times, I used the same machine to clear the topsoil and dig out the cellar for the church. The 310E is a superb machine, very well designed and built, easy to operate and easy to maintain. We have a similar machine on our ranch in Wyoming.

Of the various skills I have learned, flying has been the most useful, the most rewarding, and the most enjoyable. Not only did I completely shed my fear of being airborne, but the convenience of self-transport is transformative. Weather permitting, you can leave just when you want, and finishing your activity at the destination, you can return just when you want. Only at certain foreign airports are you ever hindered by the security procedures that most commercial passengers must endure. Being my own pilot also relieves me of the added cost of a crew, their salaries and travelling expenses.

Most people assume that learning how to fly is difficult. It really is not. I discovered early on that only about 10 percent of what you learn relates to controlling the aircraft and making proper use of the avionics. The other 90 percent consists primarily of learning how to exercise proper judgment: how to evaluate the weather, how to evaluate the condition of the aircraft, how to interpret the regulations promulgated by the FAA, when and how to report unusual situations to ATC such as turbulence or observed air traffic. And there is very little math involved. I have so far logged over 11,500 hours in both airplanes and helicopters. This represents more than 1.31 years of my life spent airborne. With luck and good health, I will be able to continue for years to come.

I think you would have to agree, Dear Reader, that I should not yet count writing as one of my skills. However, I shall endeavor to improve its quality in the future.

I have found, over the years, that working to develop skills of whatever nature is a worthwhile life pursuit. How can one ask for others to perform work if one is not willing to work oneself? Work of whatever kind is itself noble; it gives real meaning and value to the rewards which are therefrom derived. And it starkly illuminates the tragedy of those who are bribed to not work in exchange for a government-sponsored dole. Whether rich or poor, how can any individual derive satisfaction from being an inert bystander, without purpose, without ambition, and without the tremendously rewarding feeling that comes from doing something worthwhile?

CHAPTER XXV

SLAVERY REDUX

Which just happens to remind me of my political beliefs . . . .

My grandparents, I am sure, all considered themselves to be Republicans. My parents were Republicans. They certainly tried to teach me values that today would be considered to be based on principles espoused by the Republican Party.

Growing up, I don't remember giving politics much thought. When I matriculated at Yale in the fall of 1960, I found myself in the midst of the Kennedy-Nixon presidential election. The famous televised debate left me with the vague impression that Kennedy was the candidate of greater intelligence and integrity. Nixon came off as a sleaze-ball. But it really didn't matter that much to me at the time because the voting age had not yet been lowered to eighteen.

Kennedy's victory signaled the beginning of a tumultuous era. The Berlin Wall. Governor Wallace standing in the school house doorway attempting to thwart the very advance of history and civil rights. Khrushchev sent his missles to Cuba and blinked only at the very last moment so as to save the planet from destruction. Dieter was hell-bent on surviving, of course, but the rest of us were figuratively hiding under our desks. Then the assassinations: JFK, RFK, MLK. All this as a nascent conflict in Vietnam began to suck us all into an endless whirlpool of tragedy and uncertainty.

I remember my father telling the story of he and Bunny going to the Post Office in Upperville to vote in the presidential election of 1960. "Paul, may I please borrow your pencil to complete my ballot?" "**You're going to vote for Nixon, aren't you?**" "No, I'm going to vote for Kennedy." **"Then no, you can't borrow my pencil!"** So by this time, there was a break in the ranks. My stepmother went on to befriend the Kennedys, to the point where she was asked by Jackie to redesign the Rose Garden at the White House. The Kennedys were from time to time invited to our house on Cape Cod during the summer. I remember the President carelessly allowing a long cigar ash to fall onto the living room shag carpet. "Don't worry, Sir," I blurted, "I'll take care of that."

Things were not going well in the World. It was only natural to gravitate towards a Liberal viewpoint, especially with respect to the civil rights crises that seemed to pop up all around. This was an issue over which one had to choose sides, and the moral exigency of delivering on the equality promised by the country's founders in the Declaration of Independence and in the Constitution just had no countervailing argument of any consequence. Not that I don't appreciate States' Rights.

So I voted for Lyndon Johnson in 1964. Sue and I founded Sachem Fund which, for the most part, made grants to Liberal Causes, such as the Gray Panthers. I don't remember voting for Humphrey in 1968, but I definitely voted for McGovern in 1972 and Jimmmmee in 1976. I remember being unhappy when Ford pardoned Nixon, but at least understood the logic of wanting the country to move on. I cast my ballot in 1980 for John Anderson, the Independent.

What gradually turned my head was going into business in 1977. Connecticut was not the most business-friendly environment, and the various bureaucratic hurdles we had to surmount when starting Perma Treat (local, state and even national) put a damper on my belief that government was all that useful in its constant meddling in every sphere of life. Johnson's Great Society was producing scant evidence of improved economic conditions for those at the bottom of the opportunity ladder. Carter's WIN program was a total joke…Perma Treat was able to save considerable income tax payments due to the alternate fuel tax credit—in our case for the sale of *slabwood*! Years later, even George McGovern, who happened to own a motel in Stratford, Connecticut, complained about the ever increasing difficulty of conducting business under such regulatory strangulation.

But Ronald Reagan represented something completely different. He took only a short time to break the back of the devastating inflationary spiral that had resulted from the earlier energy crisis (for which Nixon was not without fault), from the lavish spending incurred as the result of the implementation of the Great Society programs, and the new Medicare fiscal black hole. He understood that people did best for themselves when shackled with the least amount of governmental constraints. And he was able to communicate these sensible notions to a nation that was tired of war, tired of inflation, and tired of rhetoric that promised but could not deliver. He single-handedly ended the Cold War by calling the Soviet Union's bluff with his Star Wars Initiative. I will never forget the coverage of the end of his conference with Gorbachev in Reykjavik, Iceland: Gorby trotting after Reagan in the parking lot, and Reagan just shaking his head.[1] Reagan also single-handedly made conservatism into a respectable political philosophy. I voted for Reagan's re-election in 1984.

Something had obviously gone dreadfully wrong with the Great Society and the Liberal onslaught. Poor people had become no less poor. Black people, in spite of heroic efforts by the "Establishment" to right

1 The Summit was held in 1986 at *Höfði*, the former French Consulate in Reykjavik situated above the harbor. I happened by the site in 2008, when the building was undergoing repair. I salvaged a small section of what appeared to be the corner molding, which I preserved with a small commemorative plaque. I intend to donate it eventually to the Reagan Library.

the wrongs of the past, became even more belligerent and unwilling to pitch in to improve their own situations. Drugs rose to the level of epidemic. Single parent families became more and more prevalent. The likes of Jesse Jackson and Al Sharpton pandered endlessly to fan the flames. Head Start had shown no positive results in either the improvement of scores or in the percentage retention of students in the progression of grades. Senator Moynahan (D-NY) was one of the first to recognize that the Great Society was in danger of never even arriving. He understood that the result of all these new programs was the steady drift towards an underclass of dependence. Even Bill Clinton, a decade later, conceded that the Welfare Program was encouraging people to remain on the government teat rather than providing the intended incentive to break the bonds and make the leap into securing a job and providing for one's self.

But here we are, another two decades down the road, with a record number of citizens dependent upon government largess. They have become slaves of a new Master, Uncle Sam. Slavery Redux. For delivering their votes in the Federal Elections, they are awarded with yet more and more freebies: food stamps, cell phones, WIC payments, Obamacare, and on, and on, and on. The largess is funded by the hardworking folks, fewer and fewer in number, who are too honest or too proud to allow themselves to sink into this morass.

The entire educational system has become part of the scam: the teachers' unions perpetuate shoddy performance and foster changes in curriculum that emphasize the benefits of pandering and catering to the various groups that have been defined as victims of Capitalism. Black Studies, Women's Studies, LGBT Studies, they have all cluttered Higher Education with a mish-mash of meaningless tripe designed to brainwash gullible young adults into going along with the Dependency Syndrome.

The press, more and more referred to as the "Main Stream Media", aids and abets. Largely the propaganda arm of the Federal Government and the bureaucracy, it reports only that which supports the Dependency Message. Capitalism and Conservatism and Free Enterprise and Liberty are all mocked and derided, sometimes subtly, sometimes blatantly. MSNBC has become a caricature: Rachel MadCow, Ed "The Horse['s a$$]" Schultz, Chris "Haze", and Chris "Trickle Down" Matthews, contending with one another for Chief Laughing Stock and gradually sinking their pathetic little cable station into oblivion. They mistakenly take the good population of the United States for fools. The citizens, though, will be around long after MSNBC is gone and forgotten.

It's hardly worth mentioning the unions anymore, they have become so irrelevant. Once influential and powerful actors in industry and commerce, the unions have essentially ruined their own constituencies. Manufacturing was sent packing, first from the Northeast to the South, then to foreign lands. The last refuge for these scoundrels has become the representation of government employees. Even Franklin Roosevelt was astute enough to recognize that the Government could not be put in the position of bargaining with itself if it were to maintain process and order. Government employees, after all, represent just one more dependent class: their jobs depend upon politicians, for whom they vote, to subsidize ever increasing their numbers, at ever increasing salaries, for increasingly irrelevant and purposeless work.

The Connecticut Department of Transportation, for instance: used to be that one dump truck had one driver, now there is a crew of two; used to be that the trucks travelled at normal speed on the highways, now they crawl along at 10 miles per hour on the shoulder in order to extend the time to arrive on station and return to base; used to be that one tractor mowed the grass on the sides of the freeway, now each tractor is "protected" by two trailing dump trucks, each flashing an arrow and each carrying one of those huge rear collision bumpers. School busses also sport a crew of two. We pay for all this nonsense.

It is obvious that these trends cannot last forever. So found the Soviet

Union, which collapsed predictably into a rag-tag group of non-viable third-world pseudo nations. PIIGS in Europe (referring to Portugal, Italy, Ireland, Greece and Spain) memorializes the failure of the Euro-community to come to grips with the inevitable crunch of spending more than earning. They should have hired ex-Governor Florio from New Jersey to help them reach the inevitable conclusions. As Margaret Thatcher quipped, "The trouble with Socialism is that eventually you run out of other people's money."

How many times does history have to repeat itself before such fundamental lessons are learned? And not just learned, but actually heeded? We live in an era wherein not only are these lessons ignored, but those in "leadership" positions are trying to reinforce and buttress the falsehoods and malpractices that have brought us to this point of acute danger. The American people, in my humble opinion, will not lie quiescent forever.

It took Abraham Lincoln and the Republican Party to deal with the first scourge of slavery. And now it appears that it is again up to the Republican Party to deal with the contemporary counterpart. The question is: Is the Republican Party up to it this time?

CHAPTER XXVI
FAITH

I have never been a particularly religious person, in the sense of belonging to a denomination or attending church on any regular basis. But I do consider myself a person of Faith, a believer in an Almighty Power and Creator of everything we know (and of everything we don't know).

Religion was a part of the curriculum at Fenn School and at Milton Academy. But my starkest memory, unfortunately, was not very inspirational. In seventh grade, at the Episcopal Church in Concord, I sat one pew in front of Henry Briggs, a classmate from New York. Henry's breakfast apparently didn't agree with the sermon and found itself all over Henry and his pew. The stench pervaded the entire building through the heating ducts, such that even the Sunday School class downstairs had to be abandoned.

There is something about the institutions of religion that has never sat well with me. Perhaps it is the notion that one has to be "preached to" that seems somewhat condescending. I have always been of the opinion that the dichotomy between right and wrong is not all that difficult a concept to grasp. Why need it be explained over and over, to the point of tedium? And the Christian concept of love as contrasted to hate, perhaps a little harder to grasp at first, but certainly not comprehensible to only those with a PhD.

Over the millennia, organized religions do not have sterling records.

Christianity split between Roman and Eastern, then between Catholic and Protestant, then between traditional and Born Again. None of these offshoots are without their own faults. Christianity in the Middle Ages became a dominant controlling institution, with no checks on its behavior. The accumulation of wealth by the Church itself certainly did not comport with the Christian concepts of giving and sharing. Abusive behavior by priests that has come to light in the past half century (I call it "Club Ped") has brought the establishment to a new nadir.

And the Muslims. Shiites versus Sunnis. The Druze, the Zoroastrians, the Baha'i, and all the other offshoots. Who will rule the next Caliphate? Sectarian violence has plagued these various Believers since Muhammad passed away. I consider possible reconciliation between them as being nothing but a mirage. Yet meanwhile the adherents battle on in timeless struggles that neither permit the advancement of their welfare, nor the spiritual arrival to a world of peace.

When I observe the beauty of Nature, just outside my window, and stretching in all directions, I find it impossible to attribute it to anything but a Divine Power. The structure of sub-atomic particles versus the vastness of the Universe represent scales so divergent and miraculous as to discount any other possibility for their co-existence. The abundance and diversity of species cannot lead a person to any other conclusion but that a Mastermind has been responsible. Darwin and Pavlov can only have been part of the Plan.

Our Borgund stave church reflects, in a way, the beauty and majesty of the Universe. It soars skyward with roofs of ever diminishing size, lending to the impression of infinite recession. The sheathing shingles, shaped to a point, remind one of so many creatures of the sea. To sit in its presence whether inside or outside commands awe and respect: for the original designers, for the current builders, for the heritage it represents, and for the Deity it honors.

So when we see all the troubles that afflict the World, I believe that we have to recognize that they are part of some larger Purpose. If you would for a moment consider Humanity in the same manner as you might think of a colony of ants, then you might agree that the will and purpose of each individual may have purpose in the survival of the colony, but also that the colony has its own collective purpose to survive and thrive. In this context, I believe that Humanity will never self-destruct, that Humanity will always find solutions to the new challenges it confronts, and that Humanity will strive for its own Perfection in the long run. Otherwise, I cannot see any reason for us being here.

Mankind has experimented and used a series of institutions in its brief existence. The tribe more or less fell by the wayside when it could not provide sufficiently for its members. The Church was effective for centuries because it was able to organize the population around common goals and values. The Nation State came to the fore when the Church began to decay from the inside. And now the Nation State is fast becoming obsolete due to the rapid advance in Globalization and the revolution in communications. But I don't think this trend will inevitably lead to World Government or a plague of Black Helicopters.

Instead, I see a World in which individuals are able to form new groups based on common interest, using communications as a binding element, and pursuing these various interests (some good, and probably some not so good) to advance the well-being of their group. We are now blessed with a World of Common Knowledge: available at our fingertips with the likes of *Google,* we can research, and invent, and synthesize to an extent heretofore unimaginable. And every new product and idea becomes available to everyone else, such that the speed in the advancement of ideas will inevitably continue to escalate. The challenge for Mankind will become one of keeping up with this new pace.

I am firmly of the belief that the Winner of this new paradigm will be the Good that comes from Understanding. Self-education will become the norm; Good ideas will push out the Bad; Humanity will achieve a level of Consciousness that will preclude Evil.

CHAPTER XXVII
OUTLOOK

My life started in 1942 in the midst of an awful global conflict. Thank God, the good guys won. I have been inspired by, and tremendously thankful to, all those brave warriors that never returned from World War II. I have visited the various US cemeteries at Colleville-sur-Mer in Normandy, Épinal in the Vosges, Cambridge in England, and Carthage in Tunisia. Those that survived, of course, and those that fought in Korea, in Vietnam, in Afghanistan and Iraq are equally deserving of our respect and gratitude. As are all those from earlier conflicts, World War I, the Civil War and the War of Independence. "Freedom is not free." A lesson we must remember over and over, lest we become complacent.

It can become disheartening to consider what the current regime has done, and continues to do, to weaken our self-respect and our resolve to maintain the freedoms and liberties so hard fought for by those who preceded us. America is a great country. It is still the greatest country in the World. And I believe it will remain great, in spite of current misdirection of efforts, in spite of evidence of our bureaucracy becoming corrupted, and in spite of the incompetence that manifests itself day after day by the "leadership". The citizens of the United States of America will put up with such obviously destructive tendencies for only so long before they will rise up and object. The tools provided us in the Constitution allow for a significant majority to set right whatever is perceived to be going astray. The process of Amendment has been used many times before, and surely it will be used again. And then there is also the possibility of a Constitutional Convention.

The disturbing aspect of government in the past few decades is the propensity for those governing to not play by the rules that they have sworn to uphold. Teddy Kennedy cheated in his Spanish class at Harvard. Teddy Kennedy cheated again at Chappaquiddick, perhaps in more ways than one. (I hesitate to point out that he was also a graduate of Milton Academy.) Is it any wonder, then, that his admirers would resort to the same types of behavior? We can blame it on the parents. We can blame it on the teachers. We can blame it on the crumbling of the Church. In the end, though, we are all to blame, because if each and every one of us does not object whenever we see such shortcomings in others (or in ourselves) then we are merely aiding and abetting the wrongdoing.

It can't be easy being a saint. For sure, I'll never get there. I remember a kid named Allen Drew at Fenn School (or was it Drew Allen?) He always got an A+ in Citizenship. No matter how hard I tried, I could never break through the B+ ceiling. But over the years I think I've come to appreciate that it is the trying to get there that counts as much as anything. It is in the application of the understanding between right and wrong: if you think about it when making your choices, it helps guide you in the right direction. What can lead you astray is either false premises or irrelevant facts or simply the impatience hindering your evaluation.

In the final analysis, much also depends upon instinct. But one's instincts are really nothing more than the pattern of previous behaviors and decisions made over a lifetime. If your decisions have been good, time after time, then your instincts will propel you on the same course, kind of like an autopilot. For the most part, I feel that my record of decision making has been fairly good. But I know that relaxing and resting on one's laurels is probably the best way to run afoul of the record. Keep pondering the best way to achieve the correct course.

My life, I conclude, has been a fortunate journey. I have always enjoyed reasonably good health (save for those few short-term emergencies enumerated in Appendix B). I benefited from a first-class education. I have never been without a comfortable financial cushion, although I have always felt the need to use my own brainpower to augment what I started with. I have been fortunate in business to be associated with many fine, hard-working people who have shared my desire to be productive.[1] My family life has enriched me. I have tried to give back as much. My endeavors in life, though not all related, I hope can be judged to have moved the World forward, even if only by a small measure. I have enjoyed overcoming each and every challenge that has been placed in my path, trying in each case to multiply the good resulting from its occurrence.

Even at age seventy-two I consider my future to be bright. After my heart attack in July, 2013, I went on to a rigorous rehab program at the South County Hospital[2] in Wakefield, Rhode Island. Since then, I have tried to maintain a regiment of walking at least two miles a day (five miles on Sunday), or the equivalent amount of exercise on a treadmill or stationary bicycle. Not only do I have more energy than any time since my thirties, but I feel totally normal and up to any normal activity. I plan to return to the ski slopes soon, an activity that several years ago I abandoned due to lethargy and apprehension that I could not properly control my muscles. My diet has also improved considerably: more fruit and vegetables, more fish and shellfish. And my weight has come down

---

1 At Guilford, and then at Pan Am, we had three criteria by which to judge the desirability of our course:

1. Was it productive? 2. Was it fun? 3. Was it profitable? (In that order)

2 Thanks again to Delaine, Anne Marie and Roberto for their guidance.

from 226 to 190 pounds, my cholesterol count is down to 152. And so long as I can pass the “Bruce Protocol” Stress Test (which I must now take annually) then I will be able to continue to pilot my aircraft.

Appendix A

1 9 9 6 I T I N E R A R Y 03.19.96

N7TK Around-the-World Trip

Arrival			Time Dif	City	ICAO	Ni	Departure			NM
UDate	UTC	Locl					UDate	UTC	Locl	
			-5	Westerly, RI	KWST		01.12	1658	1158	870
01.12	1926	1556	-3.5	Gander, NL	CYQX		01.12	2010	1640	1737
01.13	0128	0128	0	Shannon, Ireland	EINN	1	01.15	1008	1008	1279
01.15	1411	1511	1	Tunis, Tunisia	DTTA	3	01.18	0827	0927	1508
01.18	1247	1447	2	Damascus, Syria	OSDI	3	01.21	0728	0928	1447
01.21	1110	1510	4	Muscat, Oman	OOMS	3	01.24	0556	0956	1407
01.24	1051	1621	5.5	Madras, India	VOMM	3	01.27	0634	1204	1133
01.27	1053	1753	7	Phuket, Thailand	VTSP	4	01.31	0607	1307	939
01.31	0920	1620	7	Hanoi, Vietnam	VVNB	5	02.05	0234	0934	504
02.05	0420	1220	8	Macao	VMMC	2	02.07	0643	1443	1463
02.07	1210	2010	8	Kuching, Malaysia	WBGG	3	02.10	0115	0915	736
02.10	0407	1207	8	Bali, Indonesia	WRRR	3	02.13	0202	1002	964
02.13	0534	1504	9.5	Darwin, Australia	YPDN	1	02.13	2304	0834	1735
02.14	0528	1628	11	Sydney, Australia	YSSY	2	02.15	2151	0851	1155
02.16	0147	1447	13	Dunedin/Queenstown	NZDN	4	02.19	2214	1114	679
02.20	0020	1320	13	Aucklnnd, NZ	NZAA	2	02.21	2046	0946	1635
02.22	0220	1620	-10	Rarotonga, Cook	NCRG	1	02.22	1947	0947	623
02.22	2153	1153	-10	Papeete, Tahiti	NTAA		02.23	2257	1257	143
02.23	2338	1338	-10	Bora Bora	NTTB	3	02.25	1921	0921	1058
02.25	2235	1335	-9	Totegegie, Gambier	NTGJ	1	02.26	1639	0739	1409
02.26	2119	1619	-5	Easter Island	SCIP	2	02.28	1238	0738	2035
02.28	1859	1559	-3	Santiago, Chile	SCEL	1	02.29	1126	0826	1364
02.29	1647	1147	-5	Lima, Peru	SPIM	1	02.29	1805	1305	1440
02.29	2311	1711	-6	San Jose, CR	MROC	1	03.01	1515	0915	1328
03.01	1939	1439	-5	Ft. Lauderdale, FL	KFXE	1	03.02	0043	1943	1038
03.02	0350	2250	-5	Westerly, RI	KWST	Total trip length:29,629 nm				

[All dates UTC; Local date one day off]

APPENDIX B

MEDICAL HISTORY

1946—Pneumonia (Washington, DC)

1948—Pneumonia (Palm Beach, FL)

1953—Ear drained of fluid (Mass. Eye and Ear Infirmary)

1954—Tonsils removed (Mass. Eye and Ear Infirmary)

1968—Osteochondroma removed (Doctors Hospital, New York)

1971—Polyp removed from sinus (Doctors Hospital, New York)

1995—Broken leg repaired (Lawrence & Memorial, New London)

2008—Prostate removed (Bay State Hospital, Springfield, MA)

2013—Stent (L&M) and quadruple bypass after heart attack (Yale—New Haven Hospital, New Haven, CT)

2014—Indirect inguinal hernia repaired (L&M)

2015—Other indirect inguinal hernia repaired (L&M)

APPENDIX C

FAVORITE MOVIES

1. *Casablanca*
2. *The Counterfeit Traitor*
3. *The Heroes of Telemark*
4. *Five Graves to Cairo*
5. *The Thirty-Nine Steps*
6. *My Cousin Vinny*
7. *Dr. Strangelove*
8. *Stalag 17*
9. *Touch of Evil*
10. *Twelve O'Clock High*
11. *The Bridges at Toko-Ri*
12. *The Treasure of the Sierra Madre*
13. *The Maltese Falcon*
14. *Summer of '42*
15. *To Catch a Thief*
16. *The Bridge on the River Kwai*
17. *Rear Window*
18. *Shane*
19. *Fargo*
20. *The Mouse That Roared*